Social Issues
in Literature

Industrialism in
John Steinbeck's
The Grapes of Wrath

Other Books in the Social Issues in Literature Series:

Social Issues
in Literature

Industrialism in John Steinbeck's *The Grapes of Wrath*

Louise Hawker, Book Editor

GREENHAVEN PRESS
A part of Gale, Cengage Learning

GALE
CENGAGE Learning

Detroit • New York • San Francisco • New Haven, Conn • Waterville, Maine • London

Christine Nasso, *Publisher*
Elizabeth Des Chenes, *Managing Editor*

© 2008 Greenhaven Press, a part of Gale, Cengage Learning

Gale and Greenhaven Press are registered trademarks used herein under license.

For more information, contact:
Greenhaven Press
27500 Drake Rd.
Farmington Hills, MI 48331-3535
Or you can visit our Internet site at gale.cengage.com

For product information and technology assistance, contact us at

Gale Customer Support, 1-800-877-4253
For permission to use material from this text or product, submit all requests online at
www.cengage.com/permissions

Further permissions questions can be emailed to permissionrequest@cengage.com

Articles in Greenhaven Press anthologies are often edited for length to meet page requirements. In addition, original titles of these works are changed to clearly present the main thesis and to explicitly indicate the author's opinion. Every effort is made to ensure that Greenhaven Press accurately reflects the original intent of the authors. Every effort has been made to trace the owners of copyrighted material.

Cover image © The Library of Congress.

ISBN: 978-0-7377-4034-9 (hardcover)
ISBN: 978-0-7377-4035-6 (paperback)

Library of Congress Control Number: 2008925249

Printed in the United States of America
1 2 3 4 5 6 7 12 11 10 09 08

Contents

Chapter 1: The Background of John Steinbeck

   Steinbeck's formative years in a poor family in the Salinas Valley of California formed the basis of his literary
   focus on the problems of common people and their
   struggles to overcome economic and social obstacles.

   Steinbeck's first-hand experience in observing and living
   in the migrant camps aroused his emotions and provided
   content, albeit controversial, for *The Grapes of Wrath*.

   Steinbeck received the Nobel Prize in 1962, a recognition
   of his literary contributions describing the lives and
   struggles of ordinary people against external forces, and
   his ability to convey both the humor and pathos of their
   plight.

Chapter 2: *The Grapes of Wrath* and Industrialism

   Beach states that *The Grapes of Wrath* reveals Steinbeck's
   sympathy for the common people who endure hardships
   and discrimination at the hands of big business and the
   capitalist system.

Chapter 3: Contemporary Perspectives on Industrialism

The Inter-American Commission on Human Rights should investigate conditions among Florida's farm workers, eliminate discrimination against farm workers in existing labor laws, and hold corporate purchasers accountable for knowingly purchasing products produced under conditions that violate human rights.

Introduction

When John Steinbeck wrote the closing passages of *The Grapes of Wrath* in 1938, it is doubtful that he was prepared for the firestorm of criticism his great novel would soon unleash. Steinbeck's portrayal of the migrants, personified by the Joads, and their exploitation at the hands of the corporate farmers, was based on his own experiences and observations in California. He was dismayed and moved by the conditions he witnessed in the field. In fact, *The Grapes of Wrath* was not Steinbeck's first foray into the world of migrant workers. *In Dubious Battle*, published in 1936, portrayed the work of political organizers in the apple fields.

But even before *The Grapes of Wrath* was published, rumors that Steinbeck was a dangerous revolutionary surfaced. A friend and bookstore owner even reported that men claiming affiliation with J. Edgar Hoover and the FBI questioned her about Steinbeck and his political views. As reported by biographer Jay Parini in *John Steinbeck: A Biography*, Steinbeck was warned to be careful because a powerful farmers' organization was out to "get him" any way they could.

In the context of the United States in the twenty-first century, with its highly industrialized and automated economy, it may be difficult to understand how the publication of a novel based on real and verifiable circumstances could generate such a backlash. But when *The Grapes of Wrath* is viewed against the backdrop of the socioeconomic climate of the 1930s, the issues become more apparent.

In 1939, the United States was still in the grip of the Great Depression, an economic collapse that continued until the early 1940s and the nation's entry into World War II. Thousands of people had lost their jobs, homes, and savings.

Many farmers of the southern United States and the Plains states experienced an even more profound change. Their entire way of life as tenant farmers was becoming a relic of the pre-industrial era. Tenant farmers lived and worked on land they did not own, typically exchanging the crops they raised for a roof over their heads. According to the Oklahoma Historical Society, tenant farmers comprised more than 60 percent of that state's farming population in the 1930s.

The advent of mechanized farming made thousands of farm workers dispensable to the farm owner. As embodied in the tractor men of *The Grapes of Wrath*, the tractor "turns the land and turns us off the land." Over-plowed and over-grazed lands were a ripe target for the drought and massive dust storms of the Dust Bowl that drove farmers from their land to the promise of prosperity in California's fertile valleys. Unlike shopkeepers or skilled tradesmen who could return to their occupations once the economy rebounded, tenant farmers were left adrift, without marketable skills, largely as a result of industrialism.

Upon their arrival in California, the migrants, known as "Okies," were once again victimized by—or at least unprepared for—an agricultural economy that was becoming more industrialized and less dependent on one's relationship to the land. The advent of fertilizers, irrigation systems, refrigeration, and other technological advances made it possible for corporate farms to grow and sell massive quantities of fruits and vegetables. In many cases, the migrants were just another commodity required to ensure efficient production and profitability.

Rather than finding salvation in California, the migrants encountered conditions similar to those they had left behind: poverty, struggle, and impersonal treatment by corporations. Having lived and worked among migrant workers for a time, Steinbeck was dismayed by their living conditions, noting the vast number of workers who, despite long hours in the fields, could not earn enough to feed their families. Tensions between the farm workers and the owners ran high and, as Steinbeck explained in his newspaper articles written before *The Grapes of Wrath*, the migrants also encountered hostility from local people. Residents reacted negatively to the invasion of these hordes of strangers and their makeshift camps. In his biography of Steinbeck, Parini quotes the author's newspaper reporting on the subject: "The hatred of the stranger occurs in the whole range of human history, from the most primitive village farm to our own highly organized industrial farming."

The corporations that operated the farms were not receptive to having newspapers expose the shortcomings of their labor management, nor did they view the publication of *The Grapes of Wrath* as a positive development. Steinbeck wrote about the animosity his novel was generating in 1938, even before it landed on bookshelves: "The vilification of me out here from the large landowners and bankers is pretty bad. The latest is a rumor started by them that the Okies hate me and have threatened to kill me for lying about them. I'm frightened at the rolling might of this damned thing. It is completely out of hand; I mean a kind of hysteria about the book is growing that is not healthy."

Soon after the publication of *The Grapes of Wrath*, some of Steinbeck's critics published responses to the novel that asserted Steinbeck had exaggerated the conditions of the migrant workers. These responses, in contrast to the novel, asserted that most migrants experienced humane treatment and relative prosperity.

For every critic of *The Grapes of Wrath*, however, there are at least as many defenders. It has been heralded as the flagship novel of the Great Depression, a classic in American literature. It has been defined as an allegory, a story of spiritual struggle intended to convey a universal message.

As a number of biographers and literary critics have noted, Steinbeck had an almost lifelong fascination with the ability of organisms, including humans, to unite and work as a single organism for the greater good. This theme is central to *The*

Grapes of Wrath. The Joads and other Okies band together as an extended family to care for and defend one another in the face of a seemingly indifferent, industrialized behemoth.

So it is fitting, perhaps, that Steinbeck's greatest literary success served to unite those who championed the causes of workers' rights and migrant welfare. In doing so, Steinbeck also exposed a dark and tumultuous era in American history to the light of public scrutiny.

Chronology

1902

John Ernst Steinbeck is born on February 27, in Salinas, California, to John Ernst Steinbeck, Sr. and Olive (Hamilton) Steinbeck. He is the only son and third born of four children.

1915

Steinbeck enters Salinas High School, a year younger than most of his classmates as a result of skipping fifth grade.

1918

Steinbeck becomes gravely ill with pneumonia as a result of the flu epidemic that swept the nation. His lungs will remain vulnerable for the rest of his life.

1919

Steinbeck graduates from Salinas High School in June and enrolls in Stanford University starting in the fall term. He attends college sporadically for the next six years.

1920

Steinbeck's father arranges for his summer job with Spreckels, a sugar company, as a maintenance man. Steinbeck meets the Mexican workers who eventually play a role in his novel *Tortilla Flat*.

1925

Steinbeck leaves Stanford University and heads for New York City, working as a hand on a ship headed through the Panama Canal. In New York City, he initially finds a job as a construction laborer and eventually as a reporter for the *New York American* newspaper.

1926

Fired from his newspaper job, Steinbeck returns to California and moves to Lake Tahoe to work as caretaker for a summer home. The Lake Tahoe area becomes his home for several years.

1929

Steinbeck publishes his first novel, *Cup of Gold,* and meets Carol Henning, who provides his first introduction to the socialist movement and left-wing politics of the day.

1930

Steinbeck marries Carol Henning, whose politics and social conscience heavily influence the author and his work throughout the 1930s. The Steinbecks, nearly broke, move to Pacific Grove, California, where Steinbeck meets marine biologist Edward F. Ricketts, who becomes his closest personal friend for two decades.

1932

Steinbeck publishes *Pastures of Heaven*; the Dust Bowl begins in the American Midwest.

1933

Steinbeck publishes *To a God Unknown.*

1935

Steinbeck experiences a turning point in his career with the publication of *Tortilla Flat,* which becomes a major success and launches a long friendship with editor Pascal Covici of Covici-Friede.

1936

Steinbeck publishes *In Dubious Battle* and writes a series of articles on migrant workers, based on personal experience, for the *San Francisco News.*

1937

Steinbeck publishes *Of Mice and Men* and *The Red Pony*. He makes his first trip to Europe and Russia. *Of Mice and Men* opens as a play.

1938

Steinbeck writes *The Grapes of Wrath* in one hundred days between June and October, succumbing to exhaustion at the end of that period. He buys his ranch in Los Gatos, California; he also receives the New York Drama Critics Circle Award for the play *Of Mice and Men*.

1939

The Grapes of Wrath is published and inspires both praise and criticism.

1940

The Grapes of Wrath earns Steinbeck the Pulitzer Prize and National Book Award. Film versions of this novel and *Of Mice and Men* are released. In all, seventeen of his works are eventually made into movies. Steinbeck and his marine biologist friend Ricketts make a research trip to the Sea of Cortez.

1941

Steinbeck and Ricketts publish *Sea of Cortez*, a study of the fauna in the Gulf of California.

1942

Steinbeck publishes *The Moon is Down*. The film version of *Tortilla Flat* is released.

1943

Steinbeck and Carol Henning divorce. Steinbeck marries Gwendolyn Conger.

1944

Steinbeck's first son, Thomas (Thom), is born.

1945

Steinbeck and Gwendolyn Conger move to New York City. *Cannery Row* is published. The film version of *The Moon is Down* is released. Steinbeck travels to Europe and North Africa as a war correspondent for the *New York Herald-Tribune*.

1946

Steinbeck's son John IV is born.

1947

The Wayward Bus and *The Pearl* are published. Steinbeck tours Russia with photographer Robert Capa.

1948

Steinbeck publishes *A Russian Journal*. He is elected to the American Academy of Letters. The film version of *The Pearl* is released. In a tumultuous year, Ed Ricketts dies, and Steinbeck and his second wife Gwendolyn Conger divorce.

1950

Steinbeck publishes *Burning Bright*, which also opens as a play, and writes the script for *Viva Zapata!* He marries his third wife, Elaine Scott.

1951

Steinbeck publishes *Log from the Sea of Cortez*.

1952

East of Eden is published; the film version of *Viva Zapata!* is released.

1954

Steinbeck publishes *Sweet Thursday*, a sequel to *Cannery Row*.

1955

The Richard Rodgers and Oscar Hammerstein musical *Pipe Dream*, based on *Sweet Thursday*, opens in New York City. The film version of *East of Eden*, starring James Dean, is released.

1957

The Short Reign of Pippin IV is published and the film version of *The Wayward Bus* is released.

1958

Steinbeck publishes *Once There Was a War*.

1959

Steinbeck travels through England and Wales, conducting research for a modern English version of Thomas Malory's *Morte d'Arthur*.

1960

Steinbeck visits forty states as he travels across America with his dog Charley, a poodle.

1961

Steinbeck publishes *The Winter of Our Discontent*.

1962

Steinbeck receives the Nobel Prize for Literature in Stockholm; *Travels with Charley* is published.

1963

Steinbeck travels to Scandinavia, Eastern Europe, and Russia, where he is very popular and his work is quite well known.

1964

Steinbeck is awarded the United States Medal of Freedom.

1965

Steinbeck covers the Vietnam War for Long Island *Newsday*.

1966

America and the Americans, a series of travel essays with blunt commentary by Steinbeck, who is quite ill, is published.

1968

Steinbeck dies on December 20 and is buried in Salinas, California.

1973

The Martha Heasley Cox Center for Steinbeck Studies is dedicated at San Jose State University.

1974

The Steinbeck House restaurant opens in Salinas, in the author's boyhood home, restored and replete with Steinbeck memorabilia.

1975

Steinbeck: A Life in Letters, is published, with Elaine Steinbeck and Robert Wallsten as editors.

1983

The Steinbeck Center Foundation is started in Salinas.

1989

Working Days: The Journals of "The Grapes of Wrath," is published, edited by Robert DeMott.

1990

Gary Sinise stars as Tom Joad in a new stage adaptation of *The Grapes of Wrath*.

1991

Thomas Steinbeck dies. The dramatization of *The Grapes of Wrath* wins the New York Drama Critics Circle Award.

1992

A film version of *Of Mice and Men*, starring Gary Sinise and John Malkovich, is released.

1993

Steinbeck's *Zapata: A Narrative in Dramatic Form on the Life of Emiliano Zapata* is published.

1998

The National Steinbeck Center opens.

2003

Elaine Steinbeck dies.

2007

Steinbeck is inducted into the California Hall of Fame, represented by his son John IV.

The Background of John Steinbeck

The Life of John Steinbeck

Richard Astro

Richard Astro is University Distinguished Professor in English and Philosophy at Drexel University in Philadelphia. In addition to his books on Steinbeck, he has authored and/or edited books on Ernest Hemingway, Bernard Malamud, and the literature of New England.

In the following viewpoint, Richard Astro explains that Steinbeck's body of work is best remembered for its focus on ordinary people battling forces—economic, social, or personal— that are larger than they are. He often promoted the concept, asserts Astro, that individuals have the capacity to act for a greater good that transcends personal gain or interests. These beliefs were influenced by situations, places, and people Steinbeck encountered during his life. His friendship with marine biologist Edward F. Ricketts, for example, was the catalyst for Steinbeck's views about the interrelationship of all life. Astro points out that Steinbeck's talent for careful observation of people and issues was instrumental in writing the vividly detailed descriptions of farm laborers and the world of the migrant camps. Steinbeck's critics often said his human portraits were overly sentimental, but Astro explains that the enduring popularity of his work, as epitomized by The Grapes of Wrath, *has proven that his reputation as one of America's most important writers about everyday people is well-deserved.*

Throughout a career which spanned four decades, John Steinbeck was a novelist of people. His best books are about ordinary men and women, simple souls who do battle against dehumanizing social forces or who struggle against their own inhumane tendencies and attempt, sometimes suc-

Richard Astro, "John Steinbeck," *Dictionary of Literary Biography, Vol. 9: American Novelists, 1910–1945*, edited by James J. Martine, Belmont, CA: Gale Research Company, 1981, pp. 43–68. Reproduced by permission of Gale, a part of Cengage Learning.

cessfully, sometimes not, to forge lives of meaning and worth. At the center of Steinbeck's thematic vision is a dialectic between contrasting ways of life: between innocence and experience, between primitivism and progress, and between self-interest and commitment to the human community. His most interesting characters, George Milton and Lennie Small in *Of Mice and Men*, the paisanos of *Tortilla Flat*, Doc Burton of *In Dubious Battle*, Mack and the boys in *Cannery Row*, and the Joads of *The Grapes of Wrath*, struggle to resolve this personal and social conflict in a world of human error and imperfection.

In much of his work, Steinbeck championed what in *The Grapes of Wrath* he called "man's proven capacity for greatness of heart and spirit." Man, says Steinbeck, "grows beyond his work, walks up the stairs of his concepts, emerges ahead of his accomplishments." And yet, he was sensitive to "a strange duality in the human." In the narrative portion of *Sea of Cortez*, he says that man "might be described fairly adequately, if simply, as a two-legged paradox. He has never become accustomed to the tragic miracle of consciousness. Perhaps, as has been suggested, his species is not set, has not jelled, but is still in a state of becoming, bound by his physical memories to a past of struggle and survival, limited in his futures by the uneasiness of thought and consciousness."

The "tragic miracle of consciousness" is, for Steinbeck, man's greatest burden and his greatest glory. And the way in which Steinbeck portrays this burden and this glory in his novels and short stories is the source of his greatest strength as a writer. It accounts for the feeling, the passion in his fiction, as well as that feeling's extreme—sentimentality. It was his most important thematic concern, from his depiction of Henry Morgan's drive for power and wealth in *Cup of Gold* to the concluding statement in his Nobel Prize speech in which he paraphrased John the Apostle by noting that "in the end is the Word, and the Word is Man, and the Word is with Man."

Steinbeck's Modest Roots

Steinbeck was born and grew up in that long, narrow strip of agricultural land called the Salinas Valley, which is bordered on the east by the Gabilon Mountains, on the west by the Santa Lucia range, and then Monterey Bay. He was the third of four children, and the only son, of John Ernst Steinbeck II, manager of a flour mill and treasurer of Monterey County, and Olive Hamilton Steinbeck, a former teacher. Years later Steinbeck said of his youth, "We were poor people with a hell of a lot of land which made us think we were rich people, even when we couldn't buy food and were patched." As a boy he explored the valley, following the Salinas River to its mouth in Monterey Bay and visiting the towns along its shore: Monterey, Carmel, Seaside, and Pacific Grove. He loved the Corral de Tierra and was awed by Big Sur, with its sea cliffs and forests.

In the Salinas Valley, in the Corral de Tierra, and on the Monterey Peninsula and Big Sur Steinbeck found much of the material for his fiction. *Of Mice and Men, In Dubious Battle*, and *The Grapes of Wrath*, as well as many of the stories in *The Long Valley*, are set in California's agricultural valleys. The action in *Tortilla Flat, Cannery Row*, and *Sweet Thursday* takes place along the waterfront of Monterey Bay. *The Pastures of Heaven* is Steinbeck's name for the Corral de Tierra. And the mystic quality of *To a God Unknown* owes much to the strange brooding nature of Big Sur. Later in life, Steinbeck became a New Yorker, and he summered in Sag Harbor rather than in Pacific Grove. Still, central California remained to Steinbeck what [the fictional Mississippi county] Yoknapatawpha was to [American author William] Faulkner. There is an acute consciousness of place in Steinbeck's California fiction, a way of seeing which informs the thematic design of his most successful work.

Graduating from Salinas High School in 1919, Steinbeck entered Stanford University, which he attended intermittently until 1925. He had to work to pay for his education and sometimes took off one quarter to earn enough money to pay for the next quarter. He clerked in stores, worked as a surveyor in Big Sur, and was a hand on a ranch near King City, which he later used as the setting for *Of Mice and Men*. Several times he worked for the Spreckels Sugar Company, gaining firsthand knowledge of the labor problems he would write about in his political novels, *In Dubious Battle* and *The Grapes of Wrath*.

During the summer of 1923, Steinbeck took the general biology course at the Hopkins Marine Station in Pacific Grove, following an interest in marine biology that would be further stimulated in 1930 when he met marine biologist Edward F. Ricketts, whose ideas about the interrelationship of all life were to have a major impact on Steinbeck's world view, although Ricketts and Steinbeck had differing opinions on some points. . . .

The Grapes of Wrath Brings Success

The Grapes of Wrath is, without question, Steinbeck's most ambitious as well as his most successful novel. The epic scale of the book, which focuses on the struggles of the Joad family in their trek to California, as part of a band of Oklahoma tenant farmers from the Oklahoma dust bowl, enabled Steinbeck to say virtually everything he knew and felt about man and the world in which he lives. And whereas the battle in *In Dubious Battle* ends in chaos, *The Grapes of Wrath* ends in triumph mainly because of the influence of Jim Casy, a visionary ex-preacher.

Casy expresses Ricketts's holistic viewpoint in ignoring what he regards as superficial distinctions between right and wrong to arrive at a recognition of the unity of all life, which he defines as holy: "Maybe that's the Holy Sperit—the human sperit—the whole shebang," says Casy. Proceeding from a nonteleological [that things do not necessarily have a purpose] belief like Ricketts's conviction that "no valid *a priori*

John Steinbeck. National Archives and Records Administration.

[before examination or analysis] evaluation can be put on anything." Casy discards the codes of doctrinal Christianity and concludes, "There ain't no sin and there ain't no virtue. There's just stuff people do." Finally giving his life to help end the oppression of the dispossessed, he [Casy] becomes a Christ figure who directs his disciples (the Joad family) to action. His life and death serve as a catalyst which unites the Joads with the entire migrant family in the just struggle for human dignity and a decent way of life.

The Grapes of Wrath is surely underpinned by Steinbeck's working out the terms of his intellectual friendship with Ed Ricketts. But it also owes much to his friendship with Thomas Collins, to whom the book is dedicated and whose work as the manager of a migrant camp for the Farm Security Administration is chronicled in an important background piece to *The Grapes of Wrath* by Jackson J. Benson, and to a variety of other people associated with the problems of California agriculture at the time. In telling the story of the Joad family, Steinbeck fuses an agrarian idealism with the Ricketts doctrine of the unity of all life and with his personal gospel of social action. Throughout the course of the Joads' epic journey, Steinbeck chronicles the Joads' change from jealously regarding themselves as an isolated and self-important family unit to a recognition that they are part of one vast human family which, in Casy's words, "has one big soul ever'body's a part of." At the beginning of the novel, the Joads are interested solely in themselves. Tom wants only to lay "his dogs down one at a time." And Ma, whom Steinbeck describes as the citadel of the family, regards the pilgrimage only in terms of the welfare of her own family. But gradually, under Casy's tutelage, Tom, Ma, and the rest of the Joad family shift their orientation from the family unit to the migrant community as a whole, an act which is symbolically portrayed at the novel's conclusion when Ma's daughter, Rose of Sharon, gives her own milk to save a starving migrant. The Joads have keyed into a moving phalanx so that "the fear went from their faces, and anger took its place, and the women sighed with relief for they knew it was all right—the break had not come; and the break would never come as long as fear could turn to wrath." Structurally, the novel is particularly interesting because of the way in which Steinbeck portrays microcosm and macrocosm by alternating sections of the Joad narrative with intercalary chapters which universalize the Joad story. These chapters depict the land and the social conditions that the Joads encounter on their trek westward and in California.

The Grapes of Wrath Evokes Controversy

The Grapes of Wrath was an immediate bestseller. Published in April 1939, it reached the top of the best-seller list within two months and remained there throughout the rest of the year. The 1940 movie version, starring Henry Fonda and Jane Darwell, reinforced the book's popularity. It has been in print continuously and has been translated into a variety of foreign languages. It remains a classic and is on the reading lists in English classes throughout the world. Steinbeck, who had done some political writing, most notably in a pamphlet entitled *Their Blood Is Strong* (1938), a nonfiction account of the migrant labor problem in California, was attacked by a variety of civic, agricultural, and political interest groups who claimed that *The Grapes of Wrath* grossly distorted agricultural conditions in Oklahoma and in California. A national controversy grew around the book, and it was banned by some libraries and school boards. An editorial in *Collier's* magazine branded it as Communist propaganda, and it was attacked on the floor of Congress. Though Steinbeck received as much acclaim for *The Grapes of Wrath* as he did condemnation (the *Saturday Review* poll in 1940 nominated *The Grapes of Wrath* as the most distinguished novel of the year and Steinbeck received the Pulitzer Prize for it in 1940), the experience of writing the book and the controversy surrounding its reception took its toll on him. Feeling fatigue and needing a change of scene, he embarked with Ricketts on a zoological expedition, more for escape than anything else. They first considered collaborating on a handbook about the marine invertebrates of San Francisco Bay but abandoned that project in favor of a comprehensive study of the fauna of the Gulf of California, which was published in 1941 as *Sea of Cortez*. . . .

Steinbeck's Reputation Endures

Steinbeck died in December of 1968. At the time of his death he was in critical disrepute, and there were few serious scholars who did not share Harry T. Moore's feeling that in the future Steinbeck's literary status would be that of a Louis Bromfield [a novelist and conservationist] or a Bess Streeter Aldrich [early 20th century Nebraska writer]. But the years have proved Moore wrong. Important new books, articles, and conferences about his work have made it clear that Steinbeck was a major American writer who defined well the human experience.

It is impossible to predict the final fate of John Steinbeck's reputation, but it seems likely that his lasting fame will rest largely on his great novels of the American Depression. He was a product of his time and his milieu. As a novelist, short-story writer, journalist, and author of travel literature, he traveled light, unencumbered by the kinds of preconceptions which are impediments to clear vision. As he said in his introduction to the log portion of *Sea of Cortez*, "The design of a book is the pattern of a reality controlled and shaped by the mind of the writer." And the patterns Steinbeck shaped in his fiction and nonfiction are the record of a man who wanted to join in. His works differ widely in scope as well as in quality, but his canon as a whole is the record of a man who in his own time and with his own voice defined and gave meaning to the human experience. The excellence of such volumes as *The Pastures of Heaven, Tortilla Flat, Of Mice and Men,* and chiefly of *In Dubious Battle, The Grapes of Wrath,* and *Sea of Cortez* affirm that he is among the most important writers of our time.

Steinbeck's Personal Observations Informed *The Grapes of Wrath*

Peter Lisca

Peter Lisca is a literary critic who has written extensively about the life and works of John Steinbeck.

Steinbeck observed firsthand the suffering and degradation experienced by the people in California's migrant camps. His experiences in those fields, including actually living in a migrant camp for a period, provided material for a series of articles titled "The Harvest Gypsies" that appeared in The San Francisco News. *Steinbeck's compassion and righteous anger about the conditions he witnessed were incorporated into* The Grapes of Wrath. *The novel immediately provoked controversy, and the accuracy of Steinbeck's portrayals of the migrants was disputed. The book was banned and even burned in some cities. Subsequently, Steinbeck and a photographer for* Life *magazine visited migrant camps, resulting in a pictorial record that proved Steinbeck had not exaggerated the conditions he witnessed.*

Steinbeck's trek from Oklahoma to the cotton fields of California in the fall of 1937 was not the first of such forays made to observe his materials at first hand. He had made several trips into the agricultural areas of California in preparation for his strike novel, and immediately after completing *Of Mice and Men* in September of 1936 he had gone to observe the squatters' camps near Salinas and Bakersfield. There he gathered materials for "Dubious Battle in California" (*Nation*, Sept. 12, 1936) and a series of seven other articles called "The Harvest Gypsies," which appeared in the *San Francisco News*, October 5–12, 1936. On his return from his trip he wrote to

Peter Lisca, "The Grapes of Wrath," *The Wide World of John Steinbeck*, The Gordian Press. Reproduced by permission.

Ben Abramson [a bookseller and friend], "California is not very far from civil war. I hope it can be averted." He expressed the same concern to his agents: "I just returned yesterday from the strike area of Salinas and from my migrants in Bakersfield. This thing is dangerous. Maybe it will be patched up for a while, but I look for the lid to blow off in a few weeks. Issues are very sharp here now. . . . My material drawer is chock full."

During one period that autumn Steinbeck lived in one of the federal migrant camps in central California and wrote to Lawrence Clark Powell [librarian at UCLA], "I have to write this sitting in a ditch. I'm out working—may go south to pick a little cotton. Migrants are going south now and I'll probably go along." After the publication of *The Grapes of Wrath* these migrants sent Steinbeck a patchwork dog sewn from pieces of shirt-tails and dresses and bearing around its neck a tag with the inscription "Migrant John."

The *San Francisco News* articles are straight-forward reports of living conditions among migrant workers, along with suggestions and appeals for a more enlightened treatment of these people. Although they contain several details which were later incorporated in *The Grapes of Wrath*, these articles are significant primarily as a record of Steinbeck's attitude toward the people and conditions which he was to use as the materials of his great novel. Actually, the extremes of poverty, injustice, and suffering depicted in these articles are nowhere equaled in *The Grapes of Wrath*.

Steinbeck was still trying to understand the total situation. He did not go into the field to substantiate a ready-made theory. When the editors of *Occident* asked him for an article of a political nature, he refused, saying, "Generalities seem to solidify so quickly into stupidities. A writer can only honestly say—'This is the way it seems to me at this moment.'" He didn't think he knew enough about the situation and didn't wish to retire into some "terminology." Steinbeck did, however, allow the editors to print his letter of refusal, part of which follows:

> The changes go on so rapidly and it is so hard to see! Sad that it will be so easy in fifty years. Of course there is a larger picture one can feel. I suppose the appellations communist and fascist are adequate. I don't really think they are. I'm probably making a mistake in simply listening to men talk and watching them act, hoping that the projection of the microcosm will define the outlines of the macrocosm. There will come a time and that soon, I suppose, when such a position will be untenable, when we'll all put on blinders and put our heads down, and yelling some meaningless rallying cry, we'll do what men of every other time have done— tear the guts out of our own race.

Steinbeck Is Moved by Migrants' Plight

Unlike Doc in *In Dubious Battle*, however, Steinbeck's attempt to understand did not make him a dispassionate observer. In the autumn of that same year he was planning to accept a Hollywood contract of a thousand dollars a week for six weeks' work on *Of Mice and Men* so that he could give two dollars apiece to three thousand migrants. Pascal Covici [Steinbeck's editor] flew out to the coast to talk him out of it. Early in 1938, in the midst of work on the new novel, he wrote his agents, "I must go over into the interior valleys. There are five thousand families starving to death over there, not just hungry, but actually starving. . . . In one tent there are twenty people quarantined for smallpox and two of the women are to have babies in that tent this week. . . . Talk about Spanish children. The death of children by starvation in our valleys is simply staggering. . . . I'll do what I can. . . . Funny how mean and how little books become in the face of such tragedies." When *Life* offered to send him into the field with a photographer to write about the migrants, he informed his agents that he would accept no money other than expenses—"I'm sorry but I simply can't make money on these people. . . . The suffering is too great for me to cash in on it." It is this great compassion which accounts for the difference in tone between *In Dubious Battle* and *The Grapes of Wrath*.

But this compassion, this honest indignation, did not carry Steinbeck into propagandism or blind him to his responsibilities as a novelist. "The subject is so large that it scares me," he wrote. "And I am not going to rush it. It must be worked out with care." By June of 1938 he finished a sixty-thousand-word novel called *L'Affaire Lettuceberg*. To his agents and publishers, who were expecting the book and had announced it variously as *Oklahoma* and *Lettuceberg*, he sent the following joint letter:

> This is going to be a hard letter to write. I feel badly about it. You see this book is finished and it is a bad book and I must get rid of it. It can't be printed. It is bad because it isn't honest. Oh! the incidents all happened but—I'm not telling as much of the truth about them as I know. In satire you have to restrict the picture and I just can't do satire. . . . I know that a great many people would think they liked this book. I, myself, have built up a hole-proof argument on how and why I liked it. I can't beat the argument, but I don't like the book. And I would be doing Pat [his editor, Pascal Covici] a greater injury in letting him print it than I would by destroying it. Not once in the writing of it have I felt the curious warm pleasure that comes when work is going well. My whole work drive has been aimed at making people understand each other and then I deliberately write this book, the aim of which is to cause hatred through partial understanding. My father would have called it a smart-alec book. It was full of tricks to make people ridiculous. If I can't do better I have slipped badly. And that I won't admit—yet. . . .

Such a letter makes ridiculous any insinuation that Steinbeck's "social protest" was literary opportunism. It is Steinbeck's corollary to Hemingway's ideal of writing "truly," without "tricks," and without "cheating."

Steinbeck is pictured here with his wife, Elaine Andersen. Time & Life Pictures/Getty Images.

Steinbeck Works to Exhaustion

Steinbeck continued to work on his big novel all that summer, and by autumn it was in its final stages. "I am desperately tired," he wrote, "but I want to finish. And mean. I feel as though shrapnel were bursting about my head. I only hope the book is some good. Can't tell yet at all. And I can't tell whether it is balanced. It is a slow plodding book but I don't think that it is dull." On September 16, 1938, he sent Pascal Covici the book's title—*The Grapes of Wrath*—saying, "I like the soft with the hard and the marching content and the American revolutionary content." Three months later he suggested to Covici that the "Battle Hymn of the Republic" be printed somewhere in the book, possibly as end pages.

The completion of *The Grapes of Wrath*, late in 1938 left Steinbeck exhausted. He was confined to bed for some weeks and forbidden on doctor's orders to read or write. But he conscientiously saw the book through the press. As in the publication of *In Dubious Battle*, there arose the problem of printable language. Steinbeck's stand was again firm. He warned the publishers that no words must be changed; even "shitheels" must remain. Also, he refused to have included in the book a page reproduced in his own handwriting. He insisted on keeping his personality out of it. The book was to stand on its own merits, even if it meant a loss in sales. He didn't want "that kind" of reader anyway. In April, 1939, the Viking Press brought out *The Grapes of Wrath*.

The Novel Comes Under Attack

The Grapes of Wrath did not have a chance of being accepted and evaluated as a piece of fiction. From the very beginning it was taken as substantial fact and its merits debated as a document rather than as a novel. This was to be expected in a decade which had produced such motion pictures as Pare Lorentz' *The River* and *The Plow That Broke the Plains*; such books as Dorothea Lange's and Paul S. Taylor's *An American Exodus: A Record of Human Erosion*, Archibald MacLeish's *Land of the Free*, Erskine Caldwell's and Margaret Bourke-White's *You Have Seen Their Faces*, and the WPA [Works Progress Administration] collection of case histories called *These Are Our Lives*, to cite only a few. The line between social documentation and fiction has never been so hazy, and this lack of a definite line resulted in works like *Land of the Free*, which is neither an illustrated text nor a book of pictures with captions, but a form in itself. Often what was intended as social documentation and reportage had a literary value achieved only rarely in proletarian fiction—Ruth McKenney's *Industrial Valley* being an example.

Even aside from the fact that *The Grapes of Wrath* came, in such a period, Steinbeck's novel had the vulnerability of all social fiction—it was subject to attack on its facts. It is not within the scope of this study to present an exhaustive analysis either of the attack made on his facts and their defense or of the sociological and political consequences of the book, but a small sampling of the relevant literature may indicate the nature of that social-political-economic controversy which eclipsed *The Grapes of Wrath* as a novel.

Critics Dispute Portrayal of the Migrants

Within two months after the publication of *The Grapes of Wrath*, there appeared a slim volume called *Grapes of Gladness: California's Refreshing and Inspiring Answer to John Steinbeck's "Grapes of Wrath"*. This title, a remnant from the age of pamphleteering, was affixed to the story of a family of migrants who came to California poverty-stricken and found that everyone, including the banks and growers, welcomed them with open arms. They were given free land, loaned money, and lionized. In an "Addenda" to this soap opera, the author tries to break down some of Steinbeck's "facts."

Another book, *The Truth About John Steinbeck and the Migrants*, tells of its author's own experiences on a trip which he made, disguised as a migrant, just to see what conditions really were. This "migrant" found that he was able to average four dollars a day on wages and that almost all the growers begged him to stay with them and live in the ranch house all year round. In an essay which prefaces this sojourn in the land of Canaan, the author calls *The Grapes of Wrath* "a novel wherein naturalism has gone berserk, where truth has run amuck drunken upon prejudice and exaggeration, where matters economic have been hurled beyond the pale of rational and realistic thinking."

Steinbeck Documents Migrant Camps, Refutes Critics

Defenses of the book's accuracy were no less vehement. Professors of sociology, ministers, and government officials put themselves on record that Steinbeck's information was accurate. The subject was debated on radio programs such as "Town Meeting," and the book was publicly reviewed before mass audiences. Before making the motion picture, Zanuck sent private detectives to ascertain the accuracy of the novel and found conditions even worse than described by Steinbeck. The author himself, accompanied by a photographer, visited hundreds of migrant camps, took notes and made a pictorial record which was later printed in *Life*, evidence that the motion picture had not exaggerated. The book itself was both banned and burned on both political and pornographic grounds from Buffalo, New York, to California, and [New York's] Archbishop [Francis] Spellman's denunciation of it appeared in all the Hearst papers. Not the least antagonism was fomented in Oklahoma, whose native sons found themselves degraded and abused and whose bookstores found that the novel's circulation exceeded even that of *Gone With the Wind*. Oklahoma Congressman Lyle Boren denounced the book in Congress, maintaining that "the heart and brain and character of the average tenant farmer of Oklahoma cannot be surpassed and probably not equaled by any other group. . . ." He called the book itself "a black, infernal creation of a twisted, distorted mind." The Oklahoma Chamber of Commerce tried to stop the filming of the picture. No American novel since *Uncle Tom's Cabin* has created such an immediate reaction on so many levels.

Steinbeck Was Honored for Sympathetic Portrayals of the Oppressed

Anders Österling

Anders Österling was a permanent member of the Swedish Academy and long-time Nobel committee chairman. He belonged to the academy starting in 1919 and became a member of the Nobel committee in 1921.

The Swedish Academy, which bestows the Nobel Prizes, awarded its 1962 Prize in Literature to Steinbeck in recognition of his literary contributions. The academy singled out his realistic and sympathetic portrayals of the oppressed and his defense of human values throughout his works. Steinbeck was also honored for his distinctly American temperament exemplified by his feeling for nature, the tilled soil, and the geography that inspired him to depict the simple joys of life, contrasted against the greed and money-centered motives of other elements of society. The Swedish Academy concluded that Steinbeck's overriding good will toward humanity was aligned with the academy's own values and that of the Nobel Prize.

John Steinbeck, the author awarded this year's Nobel Prize in Literature, was born in the little town of Salinas, California, a few miles from the Pacific coast near the fertile Salinas Valley. This locality forms the background for many of his descriptions of the common man's everyday life. He was raised in moderate circumstances, yet he was on equal terms with the workers' families in this rather diversified area. While studying at Stanford University, he often had to earn his living by working on the ranches. He left Stanford without graduating and, in 1925, went to New York as a freelance writer. After bitter years of struggling to exist, he returned to California, where he found a home in a lonely cottage by the sea. There he continued his writing.

Although he had already written several books by 1935, he achieved his first popular success in that year with *Tortilla Flat*. He offered his readers spicy and comic tales about a gang of *paisanos*, asocial individuals who, in their wild revels, are almost caricatures of King Arthur's Knights of the Round Table. It has been said that in the United States this book came as a welcome antidote to the gloom of the then prevailing depression. The laugh was now on Steinbeck's side.

Steinbeck Writes About Serious Topics

But he had no mind to be an unoffending comforter and entertainer. The topics he chose were serious and denunciatory, as for example the bitter strikes on California's fruit and cotton plantations which he depicted in his novel *In Dubious Battle* (1936). The power of his literary style increased steadily during these years. The little masterpiece *Of Mice and Men* (1937), which is the story of Lennie, the imbecile giant who, out of tenderness alone, squeezes the life out of every living creature that comes into his hands, was followed by those incomparable short stories which he collected in the volume *The Long Valley* (1938). The way had now been paved for the great work that is principally associated with Steinbeck's name, the epic chronicle *The Grapes of Wrath* (1939). This is the story of the emigration to California which was forced upon a group of people from Oklahoma through unemployment and abuse of power. This tragic episode in the social history of the United States inspired in Steinbeck a poignant description of the experiences of one particular farmer and his family during their endless, heartbreaking journey to a new home.

In this brief presentation it is not possible to dwell at any length on individual works which Steinbeck later produced. If

Steinbeck (third from right) poses with fellow Nobel Prize winners after receiving their awards on September 10, 1962. Popperfoto/Getty Images.

at times the critics have seemed to note certain signs of flagging powers, of repetitions that might point to a decrease in vitality, Steinbeck belied their fears most emphatically with *The Winter of Our Discontent* (1961), a novel published last year. Here he attained the same standard which he set in *The Grapes of Wrath*. Again he holds his position as an independent expounder of the truth with an unbiased instinct for what is genuinely American, be it good or bad.

Strengths of *The Winter of Our Discontent*

In this recent novel, the central figure is the head of a family who has come down in the world. After serving in the war, he fails at whatever he tries until at last he is employed in the simple work of a grocery store clerk in the New England town of his forefathers. He is an honest man and he does not complain without due cause, although he is constantly exposed to temptation when he sees the means by which material success must be purchased. However, such means require both hard scrupulousness and moral obduracy, qualities he cannot muster without risking his personal integrity. Tellingly displayed in his sensitive conscience, irradiated like a prism, is a whole body of questions which bear on the nation's welfare problems. This is done without any theorizing, using concrete, or even trivial, everyday situations, which are nonetheless convincing when described with all of Steinbeck's vigorous and realistic verve. Even with his insistence on the factual, there are harmonic tones of daydreaming, fumbling speculations around the eternal theme of life and death.

Travels with Charley Assesses Progress and Society

Steinbeck's latest book is an account of his experiences during a three-month tour of forty American states, *Travels with Charley* (1962). He travelled in a small truck equipped with a cabin where he slept and kept his stores. He travelled incognito, his only companion being a black poodle. We see here what a very experienced observer and *raisonneur* [a character who speaks for the author] he is. In a series of admirable explorations into local colour, he rediscovers his country and its people. In its informal way this book is also a forceful criticism of society. The traveller in Rosinante—the name which he gave his truck—shows a slight tendency to praise the old at the expense of the new, even though it is quite obvious that he is on guard against the temptation. "I wonder why progress so often looks like destruction", he says in one place when he sees the bulldozers flattening out the verdant forest of Seattle to make room for the feverishly expanding residential areas and the skyscrapers. It is, in any case, a most topical reflection, valid also outside America.

Honored for Realistic and Imaginative Writing

Among the masters of modern American literature who have already been awarded this Prize—from Sinclair Lewis to Ernest

Hemingway—Steinbeck more than holds his own, independent in position and achievement. There is in him a strain of grim humour which, to some extent, redeems his often cruel and crude motif. His sympathies always go out to the oppressed, to the misfits and the distressed; he likes to contrast the simple joy of life with the brutal and cynical craving for money. But in him we find the American temperament also in his great feeling for nature, for the tilled soil, the wasteland, the mountains, and the ocean coasts, all an inexhaustible source of inspiration to Steinbeck in the midst of, and beyond, the world of human beings.

The Swedish Academy's reason for awarding the prize to John Steinbeck reads, "for his realistic as well as imaginative writings, distinguished by a sympathetic humour and a keen social perception."

Dear Mr. Steinbeck—You are not a stranger to the Swedish public any more than to that of your own country and of the whole world. With your most distinctive works you have become a teacher of good will and charity, a defender of human values, which can well be said to correspond to the proper idea of the Nobel Prize.

Social Issues in Literature

CHAPTER 2

The Grapes of Wrath and Industrialism

Reverence for the Common People

Joseph Warren Beach

Joseph Warren Beach (1880–1957) published numerous books of criticism as well as anthologies. He was also a published poet. Beach chaired the English Department at the University of Minnesota for many years.

At the time it was published in 1939, The Grapes of Wrath was, according to Joseph Warren Beach, a prime example of a proletarian novel, a work depicting the experience of the working class. However, rather than using a heavy-handed propaganda-laden approach, Steinbeck skillfully wove a narrative that engages the reader in the plight of the Okies—farmers from the Great Plains and Southwest regions of the United States who migrated to California in search of work—and, in particular, the Joads. Beach explains that Steinbeck promotes his social views via sympathetic characters that personify his regard for common people and their perseverance in the face of overwhelming obstacles. By dramatizing social problems through the literary art form, Beach asserts, Steinbeck gained greater emotional power and attention for the injustices and mistreatment of migrant workers.

The Grapes of Wrath is perhaps the finest example we have so far [as of 1941] produced in the United States of the proletarian novel. This is a somewhat loose term to designate the type of novel that deals primarily with the life of the working classes or with any social or industrial problem from the point of view of labor. There is likely to be a considerable element of propaganda in any novel with such a theme and

Joseph Warren Beach, "John Steinbeck: Art and Propaganda," in *American Fiction 1920–1940*, Belmont, CA: Macmillan Company, 1941, pp. 327–347. Reproduced by permission of Gale, a part of Cengage Learning.

such a point of view. And it often happens that the spirit of propaganda does not carry with it the philosophical breadth, the imaginative power, or the mere skill in narrative which are so important for the production of a work of art. Upton Sinclair is an example of a man of earnest feeling and admirable gifts for propaganda who has not the mental reach of a great artist nor the artist's power of telling a plausible story and creating a world of vivid and convincing people. . . .

With Steinbeck, it is the other way round. He has been interested in people from the beginning, from long before he had any theory to account for their ways. What is more, he is positively fond of people, more obviously drawn to them than [many writers of the era]. More especially he has shown himself fond of men who work for bread in the open air, on a background of fields and mountains. They have always appealed to him as individuals, and for something in them that speaks to his esthetic sense. He sees them large and simple, with a luster round them like the figures in Rockwell Kent's engravings. He likes them strong and lusty, ready to fight and ready to make love. He likes to see the women nursing their babies. He likes to see people enjoying their food, however coarse, and sharing it with others, what there is of it. . . .

Vital Persistence of the Common People

[The final episode of *The Grapes of Wrath*, in which Rosasharn nurses a starving man with the milk intended for her child,] is symbolic in its way of what is, I should say, the leading theme of the book. It is a type of the life-instinct, the vital persistence of the common people who are represented by the Joads. Their sufferings and humiliations are overwhelming; but these people are never entirely overwhelmed. They have something in them that is more than stoical endurance. It is the will to live, and the faith in life. The one who gives voice to this is Ma. When they are driven out of their Hooverville and Tom is with difficulty restrained from violent words and acts against the deputies, it is Ma who explains to him what we might call the philosophy of the proletariat.

> "Easy," she said. "You got to have patience. Why, Tom—us people will go on livin' when all them people is gone. Why, Tom, we're the people that live. They ain't gonna wipe us out. Why, we're the people—we go on."

> "We take a beatin' all the time."

> "I know," Ma chuckled. "Maybe that makes us tough. Rich fellas come up an' they die, an' their kids ain't no good, an' they die out. But, Tom, we keep a comin'. Don' you fret none, Tom. A different time's comin'."

> "How do you know?"

> "I don' know how."

Rosasharn's gesture in the barn is not the only symbol of this will to live. Very early in the book the author devotes a whole chapter—a short one—to the picture of a turtle crossing the highway. It is an act of heroic obstinacy and persistence against heavy odds. This is a gem of minute description, of natural history close-up, such as would delight the reader of [Henry David] Thoreau or John Burroughs. There are things like this in Thomas Hardy's Wessex novels. And as in Hardy, so here—it is not a mere piece of gratuitous realism. It may be enjoyed as such. But it inevitably carries the mind by suggestion to the kindred heroisms of men and women. It sets the note for the story that is to follow.

This chapter is an instance of a technical device by which the author gives his narrative a wider reference and representative character. The story of the Joads is faithfully told as a series of particular incidents in their stirring adventure. We hang with concern and suspense over each turn of their fortunes. But the author is not content with that. He wishes to give us a sense of the hordes of mortals who are involved with the Joads in the epic events of the migration; and along with the material events he wishes us to see the social forces at play and the sure and steady weaving of new social patterns for a people and a nation. And so, to every chapter dealing with the Joads, he adds a shorter, more general, but often not less powerful chapter on the general situation.

There is, to begin with, an account of the dust storm over the gray lands and the red lands of Oklahoma—a formidable example of exact and poetic description matched by few things in fiction. Like Hardy with Egdon Heath, Steinbeck begins with physical nature and comes by slow degrees to humanity. The chapter ends with an account of the reactions of the men, women and children in the face of this catastrophe. The conception is large and noble. Humanity has been stripped of all that is adventitious [acquired] and accidental, leaving the naked will and thought of man. Under the stress of desperate calamity the children watch their elders to see if they will break. The women watch the men to see if this time they will fail. It is a question of going soft or going hard; and when the men go hard the others know that all is not lost. The corn is lost, but something more important remains. And we are left with the picture of the men on whom they all depend. It is man reduced to the simplest terms—man pitted against the brute forces of nature—man with the enduring will that gives him power to use his brains for the conquering of nature. Man's thinking is an extension of his powers of action—he thinks with his hands. . . .

A Variety of Themes

Most of these intercalary [inserted] chapters have more particular themes. There is the theme of buying cheap and selling dear—the wonderful chapter of the second-hand automobile dealers. There is the theme of social forms coming into being as occasion requires. In the roadside camps the separate families are quickly assembled into one community; and community spontaneously develops its own laws out of its own obvious needs. There is the theme of large-scale production for economy and profits—the land syndicates in California who ruin the small owners. There is the theme of spring in California—its beauty, the scent of fruit, with the cherries and prunes and pears and grapes rotting on the ground to keep up the price. There are hungry men come for miles to take the superfluous oranges; but men with hoses squirt kerosene on the fruit. "A million people hungry, needing the fruit—and kerosene sprayed over the golden mountains." And there is the theme of the blindness of property in its anonymous forms. . . .

There is the theme of a common interest as opposed to a private and exclusive one. "Not my land, but ours." "All work together for our own thing—all farm our own lan.'" And finally we have the theme of man who has lost his soul and finds it again in devotion to the common cause. . . .

Some of these themes are expressed in the spontaneous utterance of the Okies; some of them in the more abstract and theoretical language of the author. In general we may say that he is most effective when he puts his views in the mouths of the characters. For this is fiction; and fiction has small tolerance for the abstractions of an author. Still, there are cases where the theme is too broad and too complicated to find adequate expression in the words of a single man on a particular occasion. This is a great challenge to the ingenuity of a writer, and Steinbeck has found a number of ingenious and effective means of dramatizing the thought of a whole group of people faced with a difficult problem in economics. There is one remarkable chapter in which he shows us the debate between the tenant farmers and the agents of the banking syndicates come to put them off the land. It is a debate which recurs over and over again with each unfortunate family; and Steinbeck has presented it in a form that is at the same time generalized and yet not too abstract and theoretical. We are shown the farmers squatting on their heels while the owner men sit in their cars and explain the peculiar nature of the institution which they represent. It is a kind of impersonal monster that does not live on side-meat like men, but on profits. It has to have profits all the time, and ever more profits or it will die. And now that the land is poor, the banks cannot afford to leave it in the hands of men who cannot even pay their taxes. . . .

[In] a kind of parable, with allegorical figures, and with Biblical simplifications, our author has managed to give in summary, in essence, what must have gone on a million times all over the world, when the two groups were confronted—two groups that represent two opposed and natural interests, and both of them caught in an intricate web of forces so great and so automatic in their working that they are helpless to combat them or even to understand them. This is not an individual scene of drama; but many of the remarks must have been made a thousand times in individual cases. . . .

Discerning Steinbeck's Economic Theories

If I were asked to say, just exactly what are the economic theories of John Steinbeck, and how he proposes to apply them in terms of political action, I should have to answer: I do not know. The book offers no specific answer to these questions. It reminds us of what we all do know: that our system of production and finance involves innumerable instances of cruel hardship and injustice; that it needs constant adjustment and control by the conscience and authority of the sovereign people. This author is concerned with what has been called the forgotten man; it is clear that he holds the community responsible for the man without work, home, or food. He seems to intimate that what cannot be cured by individual effort must needs be met by collective measures. It is highly important that our people should be made aware of the social problems which remain to be solved within the system which is so good to so many of us. And there is no more effective way of bringing this about than to have actual instances presented vividly to our imaginations by means of fiction. For this reason I regard *The Grapes of Wrath* as a social document of great educational value.

Considering it simply as literary art, I would say that it gains greatly by dealing with social problems so urgent that they cannot be ignored. It gains thereby in emotional power. But it is a notable work of fiction by virtue of the fact that all social problems are so effectively dramatized in individual situations and characters—racy, colorful, pitiful, farcical, disorderly, well meaning, shrewd, brave, ignorant, loyal, anxious, obstinate, insuppressible, cockeyed . . . mortals. I have never lived among these Okies nor heard them talk. But I would swear that this is their language, these their thoughts, and these the very hardships and dangers which they encountered. They represent a level, material and social, on which the reader has never existed even for a day. They have lived for generations completely deprived of luxuries and refinements which in the life he has known are taken for granted as primary conditions of civilization.

And yet they are not savages. They are self-respecting men and women with a traditional set of standards and proprieties and rules of conduct which they never think of violating. Beset with innumerable difficulties, cut off from their familiar moorings, they are confronted with situations of great delicacy, with nice [i.e., very specific] problems in ethics and family policy to be resolved.

Steinbeck Was Careful Not to Sentimentalize His Characters

Louis Owens

Louis Owens was a professor at the University of California–Davis, an internationally acclaimed novelist, and a scholar of Steinbeck and Native American literature. He was one of nine children born to farm laborer parents, and he was drawn to Steinbeck because he was so familiar with the life and history of the Salinas Valley. Owens died in 2002 at age 54.

According to Louis Owens, Steinbeck was able to evoke sympathy for the Joads in The Grapes of Wrath, *while still allowing the reader to maintain some distance and perspective. Steinbeck incorporated interleaved chapters ("interchapters") that provided readers with a panorama of the cultural and socioeconomic view of the times, a device that allowed readers to distance themselves—at least partially—from the Joads' unfolding tragedy. Steinbeck also portrayed the human weaknesses and failings of the Joads, explains Owens, a technique that demonstrated their own role in the making of their fate. The Joads are shown to be as selfish and materially driven as the industrial monolith that oppresses them. These descriptions, Owens asserts, prevent the Joads from becoming overly sacrosanct and noble. Steinbeck also takes pains to illustrate that the Joads and the industrialists must share guilt and responsibility for what has happened to the land and its people.*

The Grapes of Wrath is one of John Steinbeck's great experiments, perhaps his greatest, a novel that exploded upon the American conscience in 1939, bringing home to American readers both the intimate reality of the Joads' suffer-

Louis Owens, "The Culpable Joads: Desentimentalizing *The Grapes of Wrath*," in *Critical Essays on Steinbeck's* The Grapes of Wrath, edited by John Ditsky, Belmont, CA: G.K. Hall, 1989, pp. 108–116. Reproduced by permission of Gale, a part of Cengage Learning.

ing and the immense panorama of a people's—the Dust Bowl migrants'—suffering. In spite of howls of outrage from opposite ends of the novel's journey—both Oklahoma and California—America took the Joads to heart, forming out of *The Grapes of Wrath* a new American archetype of oppression and endurance, survival if not salvation. So warmly did readers embrace the Dust Bowl Okies, in fact, that critics began almost immediately to accuse Steinbeck again of sentimentality in his portrayal of the downtrodden proletariat. . . .

As Steinbeck's most imposing and both popularly and critically successful work, *The Grapes of Wrath* has been studied from a multitude of angles, with critics focusing on its historical, political, philosophical, religious, symbolic, structural, and stylistic aspects. Steinbeck's great formal experiment in this novel—the interchapters—has been often studied and commented upon. What has been little noted in this novel, however, is the care Steinbeck takes to counterbalance the narrative's seemingly inevitable drift in the direction of sentimentalism as the story of the Joads and of the migrants as a whole unfolds in all its pathos. While Steinbeck is undeniably intensely sympathetic in this novel to the suffering of the croppers and to the plight of the seemingly powerless "little people" caught up in the destructive path of corporate America, he is at the same time painstakingly careful *not* to sentimentalize these figures, a fact of utmost importance to a critical understanding of *The Grapes of Wrath*.

Interchapters Distance Readers from the Joads

A primary means by which Steinbeck attempts to unsentimentalize this story of displacement and suffering is through his use of interchapters. As has been often noted, the most obvious value of the intercalary [inserted] chapters is to provide the big picture, to ensure the reader's awareness of the panoramic dimensions of this socioeconomic tragedy. At the same time, the narrative chapters focusing on the Joad family stem from Steinbeck's self-professed awareness that "It means very little to know that a million Chinese are starving unless you know one Chinese who is starving." Through the interchapters we feel the scope and dimension of the Dust Bowl drama; through the narrative chapters we experience the tragedy of one family on a personal, intimate level. A second very important function of the interchapters, however, one that has gone largely unnoticed, is that of offsetting the intimacy of the narrative chapters, of creating necessary distance between the reader and Steinbeck's representative family, the Joads. Steinbeck uses the interchapters skillfully as a means of preventing the reader from identifying too closely with the Joads. Again and again, just as we begin to be drawn fully into the pain of the Joads' experience, Steinbeck pulls us away from the intimate picture into the broad scope of one of the interchapters, reminding us that these are merely representative people, that the scale of suffering is so great as to dwarf the anguish of one small group such as Ma Joad's family. . . .

Both Migrants' and Oppressors' Weaknesses Shown

In addition to the depersonalizing distance achieved through the movement from narrative chapter to interchapter, Steinbeck also takes advantage of a more familiar device to desentimentalize his treatment of the downtrodden sharecropper in this novel: the objective authorial stance that he exploited so successfully in the earlier study of oppressed workers, *In Dubious Battle*. In that novel, published just three years before, Steinbeck was careful to underscore the failings of the migrant workers as well as those of the oppressors—both sides are greedy, selfish, lazy, bloodthirsty, and ignorant. These are simply aspects of the human character, says Steinbeck in that strike novel, simply the way it is, nonteleologically [without an end purpose]. In *The Grapes of Wrath*, Steinbeck does not assume the purely objective stance of the narrative voice of *In Dubious Battle*, choosing not to become "merely a recording consciousness, judging nothing" as he claimed to be in the earlier strike novel. In *The Grapes of Wrath*, Steinbeck allows his authorial voice the freedom to intrude in the guise of a modern Jeremiah [the biblical prophet], judging, condemning. However, once again in spite of his sympathies with the displaced Okies, as he did in *In Dubious Battle*, in *Grapes* Steinbeck takes care to similarly undercut the nobility and "goodness" of the migrants.

Tom, for example, is a loner who begins the novel looking out only for number one, as his solitary initial appearance and his aggressive manipulation of the witless truck driver indicate. Only gradually, through the tutoring of Casy, does the unsympathetic Tom grow into his role of proletarian savior. Throughout the novel, Pa Joad is self-centered and weak-willed, too ineffectual to assume the role of leadership demanded of him, a character thoroughly incapable of igniting the reader's sympathy, as Tom makes clear when he tells Casy late in the novel "Think Pa's gonna give up his meat on account a other fellas?" Tom's brother Al is concerned chiefly with his own concupiscence [desire] eager even near the end of the novel to abandon his family and strike out on his own with his wife-to-be. Rose of Sharon's husband, Connie, proves himself to be a selfish and soft-minded believer in the American Dream advertised in comic books and a deserter of his pregnant wife. Rose of Sharon, in turn, forces the reader to suffer through hundreds of pages of whining self-pity before her miraculous conversion near the novel's end. Even Ma, larger-than-life Earth Mother and obvious heroine of this novel, demonstrates her limitations as she rambles on pointlessly about "Putty Boy Floyd," repeating herself tediously the way real people really do as she intones one of the folkmyths of Oklahoma and the Dust Bowl region.

This family of agricultural laborers, like the Joads, traveled long distances to find work during the Depression. The Library of Congress.

While the trials of the Joads engage us, even excite our admiration and pity, Steinbeck takes pains to deny the luxury of sentimental attachment. The Joads, including even the ultimately heroic and Christ-like Casy, are no better, no greater, no less human than they should be. Nor are any of the other migrants in the novel.

Migrants Are Partly Responsible for Their Plight

More important than either Steinbeck's illumination of the human failings of his characters on such limited levels or his use of the interchapters as distancing devices is his care to emphasize the migrants' culpability, their portion of responsibility for what has happened to the land and to themselves. Certainly Steinbeck makes it clear that the sharecroppers are victimized by an inhuman economic monster that tears at the roots of Jeffersonian agrarianism [the belief that farming is the best way of life and most important industry]. However, when Steinbeck causes his representative migrant voice to plead with the owners for a chance to remain on the land, he qualifies the celebrated Jeffersonian agrarianism and love-for-the-land by tainting the croppers' wish: "Get enough wars and cotton'll hit the ceiling," the cropper argues. A willingness to accept war and death as the price for further cottoning out of the land is difficult to admire on any level. And Steinbeck goes a step further, to make it clear that the migrants are firmly fixed in a larger, even more damning American pattern. Though the tenants have tried to persuade the owners to let them hang, one hoping for a war to drive up cotton prices, the tenant-voice also warns the owners: "But you'll kill the land with cotton." And the owners reply: "We know. We've got to take cotton quick before the land dies. Then we'll sell the land. Lots of families in the East would like to own a piece of land." With their words the westering pattern of American history is laid bare: we arrive on the Atlantic seaboard seeking Eden only to discover a rocky and dangerous paradise with natives who aggressively resent the "discovery" of their land; the true Eden must therefore lie ever to the west, over the next hill, across the next plain, until finally we reach the Pacific Ocean. . . .

That the croppers are part of this pattern becomes even more evident when the representative tenant voice informs us that their fathers had to "kill the Indians and drive them away." And when the tenants add, "Grampa killed Indians, Pa killed snakes for the land," we should hear a powerful echo of the Puritan forebears who wrested the wilderness from the Satanic serpent and his Indian servants, killing and displacing the original inhabitants of the new Canaan.

It is difficult to feel excessive sorrow for these ignorant men who are quite willing to barter death to maintain their place in the destructive pattern of American expansion, a pattern that has ravaged a continent. . . .

Opening Lines Hint at Human Responsibility

The first paragraph of *The Grapes of Wrath* opens with an impressionistic swath of color reminiscent of Stephen Crane as Steinbeck intones, "To the red country and part of the gray country of Oklahoma, the last rains came gently, and they did not cut the scarred earth." He continues:

> The plows crossed and recrossed the rivulet marks. The last rains lifted the corn quickly and scattered weed colonies and grass along the sides of the roads so that the gray country and the dark red country began to disappear under a green cover. In the last part of May the sky grew pale and the clouds that had hung in high puffs for so long in the spring were dissipated. The sun flared down on the growing corn day after day until a line of brown spread along the edge of each green bayonet. The clouds appeared, and went away, and in a while they did not try any more. The weeds grew darker green to protect themselves, and they did not spread any more. The surface of the earth crusted, a thin hard crust, and as the sky became pale, so the earth became pale, pink in the red country and white in the gray country. . . .

If Steinbeck's message in the opening paragraphs is that the land cannot die, he nonetheless begins as early as the second sentence of the novel to subtly imply human responsibility for the disruption of the drought. In the second sentence, he tells us that "The plows crossed and recrossed the rivulet marks," superimposing an ultimately self-destructive human pattern—the erosion-inducing plow lines—upon the natural watershed pattern. The rivulet marks are a sign of the earth's flow, cycle, continuum; their crossing and erasure is a sign of a failure of human understanding. The wheels that "milled the ground," and the hooves that "beat the ground" until "the dirt crust broke and the dust formed" further underscores man's responsibility for the human tragedy depicted in the first paragraphs and developed throughout the novel. By the novel's end, the rain will come again in a great, destructive, cleansing flood, erasing in its turn the pattern of human failure set upon the edenic valleys of California.

Steinbeck also foreshadows in these opening paragraphs the fate of the migrants. The "weed colonies" that are "scattered . . . along the sides of the roads" suggest the colonies of migrants that will soon be scattered the length of Route 66; and the minuscule ant lion trap, a funnel of finely blown sand from which the ant simply cannot escape, serves as a naturalistic image to define the situation of the sharecroppers. They have no further [purpose] in the cropped-out region of blowing dust and sand; they have sealed their fates should they stubbornly struggle to remain. Muley Graves, whose name hints strongly at his character and fate, chooses to remain in the trap, a "graveyard ghos'" without a future.

Migrants Must Rethink Relationship with the Land

Through this burnt country cut the tracks of walking men and machines, raising dust clouds as signs of their passage. When Tom Joad appears, he will be the representative walking man, the individual who must accept responsibility for what man has done to himself and to the earth. Along with Tom, the Joads and all of the migrants will be sent on the road on a quest to rethink their relationship with humanity as well as with the land itself. What Warren French has aptly termed the "education of the heart" is a journey toward a new national consciousness, one that may, Steinbeck seems to imply, finally break the grip of the westering pattern in this country, causing Americans to free themselves from the delusive quest for a New Eden and thus from the destructive process of exploitation and removal entailed in such a pattern.

Shared Guilt and Responsibility Show New Path

Once the Joads and their fellow migrants have reached California, they can go no farther. The Joads are the representative migrants, and the migrants are the representative Americans. The migrants' westward journey is America's, a movement that encapsulated the directionality of the American experience. The horrors of the California Eden confronting the migrants have been brought on by all of us, Steinbeck implies; no one is innocent. When Uncle John releases Rose of Sharon's stillborn baby upon the flood waters with the words, "Go down an' tell 'em," Steinbeck is underscoring the new consciousness. This Moses is stillborn because the people have no further need for a *Moses*. The Promised Land has long ago been reached, and there is nowhere else to go, no place for a Moses to lead his chosen people. The American myth of the Eden ever to the west is shattered, the dangers of the myth exposed. The new leader will be an everyman, Tom Joad, who crawls into a cave of vines—the womb of the earth—to experience his rebirth and who emerges committed not to leading the people somewhere else but to making this place, this America, the garden it might be. The cleansing, destructive flood that prepares for the novel's concluding tableau rises not merely around the threatened migrants but over the entire land.

The Grapes of Wrath is Steinbeck's jeremiad [prophetic complaint], his attempt to expose not only the actual, historical suffering of a particular segment of our society, but also the pattern of thought, the mindset, that has led to this one isolated tragedy. In this novel, Steinbeck set out to expose the fatal dangers of the American myth of a new Eden, new Canaan, new Jerusalem, and to illuminate a path toward a new consciousness of commitment in place of removal, engagement instead of displacement. And in making his argument, Steinbeck was careful not to sentimentalize his fictional creations, careful to emphasize the shared guilt and responsibility—there are no innocents; a new sensibility, not sentimentality, is Steinbeck's answer.

White Okies Were Not the Only Victims of Industrialism

Charles Cunningham

This article is from Charles Cunningham's 2001 Doctoral disser-tation titled "Solidarity, Sympathy, Contempt: The Mythology of Rural Poverty in the Great Depression," published by Carnegie Mellon University.

Charles Cunningham asserts that Steinbeck ignored the non-white victims of landowners and industrialists in the migrants' story told in The Grapes of Wrath. *Many minorities also suf-fered the same oppression as the white Okies, but Cunningham states that the plight of migrant workers became valid to society as a whole only when it impacted white Americans who were considered to be "real" citizens. Steinbeck's perspective largely re-flects this silent racism. According to Cunningham, the agrarian myth of the noble Anglo-Saxon farmer permeated the culture and served only to perpetuate the exploitation of migrants from minority groups. While* The Grapes of Wrath *may be a call to socialist solidarity, Cunningham points out that the audience and the writer were in the socioeconomic middle class. However, Steinbeck does show that the white Okies will not prevail with-out collective action that includes all of the downtrodden mi-grant workers.*

Paradoxically, *The Grapes of Wrath* is both an exemplary radical analysis of the exploitation of agricultural workers and the culmination in the thirties of an implicitly racist fo-cus on whites as victims. The novel scarcely mentions the Mexican and Filipino migrant workers who dominated the California fields and orchards into the late thirties, instead im-

Charles Cunningham, "Rethinking the Politics of *The Grapes of Wrath,*" *Cultural Logic: An Electronic Journal of Marxist Theory and Practice,* vol. 5, 2002. Reproduced by permission of the author.

plying that Anglo-Saxon whites were the only subjects worthy of treatment. This focus also seems to join contemporary journalistic representations in mythologizing the Okies as quintessential American pioneers—an ideological convention that resonated with the implicit white supremacism of Jeffersonian agrarianism [the belief that farming is the best way of life and the most important industry] and of manifest destiny [a belief that the United States was destined to expand West all the way to the Pacific Ocean]. Yet, the novel also attacks the very assumptions about private property and class difference on which the social order rests ideologically. Far from being merely racist, it presents one of the most radical critiques of the social order in all of popular—and canonical [authoritative]—literature. Thus, its political intervention was—and is—contradictory. In fact, *The Grapes of Wrath* (along [with] the Okie mythology in general) arguably became a site of confrontation between the thirties anti-capitalist consciousness and the American racist tradition—between manifest destiny and manifest exploitation and dispossession.

Anticapitalism and Racism Compete

Ironically, we can see vestiges of this confrontation in comparing recent criticism of the novel with its reception in 1939. Michael Denning has lately remarked [on] the implicit racism of *The Grapes of Wrath* in his encyclopedic account of thirties left cultural production, *The Cultural Front: The Laboring of American Culture in the Twentieth Century*—a work that has been reshaping the field. For Denning, the novel is not typical of the Popular Front [PF] cultural production he celebrates, because it is imbued with "racial populism"—in contrast with what he sees as the PF's nascent multiculturalism. Yet, this is a view that was apparently unavailable to critics during the thirties, when racial essentialism [a theory that views race as a determinant of moral, cultural, and intellectual capabilities] was only recently coming to be understood as racist. They instead emphasized the novel's critique of capitalism. On the left, Granville Hicks's 1939 review in *The New Masses* declared *The Grapes of Wrath* an exemplary proletarian novel, noting that Steinbeck's "insight into capitalism illuminates every chapter of the book." He went on to remark that "No writer of our time has a more acute sense of economic forces, and of the way they operate against the interests of the masses of the people." In contrast, Denning never mentions the implicit Marxism in the novel. He is more than sympathetic with leftists, but from his point of view, the triumph of the thirties and of the Popular Front was to have working class people become cultural workers and enter the culture industries. For him, the "laboring" of American culture means that the working class came to be included as both subjects and producers of culture. Questions about what it means to be compelled to sell one's labor power or to be co-opted against one's class interests—hardly an unlikely scenario in big business cultural production—drop out of his analysis. . . .

Most people remember the cause of the Okie migration as the Dust Bowl disaster, which took place in the Great Plains states. According to this narrative, the soil literally blew away during the great drought of the mid-thirties because the plains should never have been cultivated in the first place. The resulting dust storms of topsoil left some areas buried and others denuded, generally rendering farming impossible and causing the agrarian inhabitants to have to migrate. This version was attractive to the press because the Dust Bowl and drought were spectacular and, as represented, were often uncomplicated by reference to power relations. . . .

Westward Migration Took Two Paths

It is important to note that the mythology of the Okie migration actually involved two distinct, but related problems. The outmigration of people from the Southwest, South, and upper Midwest to California was an ongoing twentieth century phenomenon that received the most public notoriety in the thirties. On the other hand, the migrant labor problem in California dated back to the mid-nineteenth century but also became famous in the thirties. As for the westward migration, [author] James Gregory notes that it came in three major phases: the teens and twenties, the Depression years, and during and after World War II. Of these three, the thirties period was perhaps the largest, and the one that concerns us here. Challenging previous assumptions, Gregory convincingly argues that refugees from the dust bowl accounted for only six percent of the southwestern migrants to California, and he reminds us that only the panhandle of Oklahoma was in the dust area (which encompassed mainly eastern Colorado, western Kansas, eastern New Mexico, and the Texas panhandle). . . .

Once in California, the story of the migration westward becomes distinct from that of the migrant farmworkers who were Okies. In general, the southwesterners tended to migrate towards the kinds of locales they had come from; city and town dwellers predominantly settled in the Los Angeles area and most of the farm people headed into the agricultural San Joaquin Valley. The latter area became the principal locus of the mythical Dust Bowl Okie and of *The Grapes of Wrath*. If the migrants began with dreams of sharing the wealth of the great agricultural valleys by eventually becoming small landowning farmers, what they found was an entrenched corporate agribusiness that mocked agrarian myths. As [author] Cletus Daniel documents, California agriculture since the latter half of the nineteenth century had been controlled by large growers who banded together in corporate cooperatives to dominate the industry. Ownership of the grower corporations often rested with banks, utilities, and other investment companies, and thus the farms themselves were often absentee-owned and managed by corporate employees. Even smaller farmers were under the sway of the large growers, because the latters' connection with the banking industry meant that they

The 1940 film version of The Grapes of Wrath *starred (from left to right) Jane Darwell as Ma Joad, Henry Fonda as Tom Joad, and Russell Simpson as Pa Joad.* © Bettmann/ Corbis.

controlled credit—a necessity for farming. The corporate growers also effectively set wages and determined the character of working conditions throughout the industry. Dissenting farmers could be bullied by banks, or sometimes squeezed out of business by large growers with vertical operations that included processing, canning, distribution, and shipping. Thus, it becomes clear that the title of Carey McWilliams's history of California agriculture, *Factories in the Field*, was not merely a simile but an apt description. . . .

Exploitable Minorities in Workforce

The ethnic makeup of the migrant workforce changed over the years, but the groups involved usually had in common that they were minorities not considered citizens of the United States—or at least *proper* citizens. As "aliens," they were thus particularly vulnerable to exploitation. Before the Civil War,

Native Americans were the first group to dominate the workforce, because the black slavery advocated by some growers was politically untenable in California. Native Americans were followed by Chinese immigrants, who were followed by the Japanese. By the 1920s, Mexicans and Mexican-Americans were the majority, with a significant Filipino minority. As Daniel recounts, growers initially felt that Mexican workers were attractive because their vulnerability would make them docile. Natives of Mexico could be readily deported at government expense and Americans of Mexican descent could be fraudulently deported. Nevertheless, this hoped-for docility quickly disappeared under the "nearly intolerable" conditions in the industry. Work stoppages and spontaneous strikes were not uncommon and intensified with the onset of the Great Depression. Growers anxious about reduced profits decided to extract the difference from workers, who responded with "angry militancy." Into this contentious situation stepped the Communist Party–sponsored Cannery and Agricultural Workers Industrial Union (CAWIU), which after faltering first steps garnered an excellent record of organizing between 1929 and 1934. The American Federation of Labor (AFL) had traditionally thought migrant labor too difficult to organize, but the majority Mexican and Filipino workers proved committed unionists.

In response both to this militancy and to the general surplus of workers produced by Depression conditions, a sentiment rose in the state to deport Mexican and Filipino workers. Anti-immigrant racism was mobilized as a false palliative [cure] for unemployment, and as a result, about one third of the Mexican and Filipino populations of the U.S. were deported or repatriated between 1931 and 1934. . . .

Migrants' Suffering Ignored

Though the conditions for field workers in California changed little in sixty or seventy years, attention to their suffering was late in coming. When the American Civil Liberties Union tried to get *The Nation* and *The New Republic*—two of the era's leading left-of-center publications—to write articles about the suspension of the constitution during the 1930 lettuce strike in the Imperial Valley, the magazines declined, believing the story minor. There was more reportage in the liberal press after the middle of the decade—McWilliams, for example, wrote several articles for *The Nation*—but it was not until the white Okies were involved that the story became nationally known. When whites were subjected to fascist conditions, the story became more than just a "labor dispute." Because mythic yeoman farmers were involved, so were the agrarian mythologies of American exceptionalism and their prerequisite white supremacism. If these quintessential Americans could be treated as badly as Mexicans and Filipinos, then Anglo-Saxon white supremacism, an ideological bulwark of US capitalism, was threatened. The worst depredations of California agribusiness had before then been concealed or sanctioned by white supremacism, which effectively blamed non-whites for their own oppression. The Okies thus highlighted the ideological contradiction between the inalienable rights of American whites to freedom and prosperity, and the rights of growers to exploit whomever they could. The Okie mythology became the site on which this struggle played out.

The contradiction the Okies posed to white supremacy was often subsumed by the "dust and drought" explanation, as we have seen in *The Plow That Broke the Plains*. This narrative saved the Okies—and the social order—from blame for their condition, because they could not be expected to control nature. The "pioneer" invocation also tended to erase the social problem by turning the Okies into symbols of America's heritage and then wishing them happily on their way. Yet, Steinbeck (like McWilliams and others) had a lot to do with keeping migrant suffering—not merely the migrant symbol—public. In his October 5–12, 1936 series of articles for the *San*

Francisco News (collected as *The Harvest Gypsies*), Steinbeck repeated the "dust and drought" explanation, but did not dwell there, choosing to focus instead on what was happening to the Okies in California. While more nuanced and politically to the left of the mainstream, the analysis in Steinbeck's series seemed to assume Anglo-Saxon white supremacism. As was true with most representations of California agricultural labor after the white workers became a majority, Steinbeck's excluded non-white workers—despite the fact that when the articles were published, the displacement of non-white workers was [as Charles Wollenberg, in his introduction to *The Harvest Gypsies* puts it,] "by no means total."

The Harvest Gypsies series articulates, in effect, a rationale for why Anglo-Saxon whites should dominate accounts of the migrant problem. . . .

No Non-whites in *The Grapes of Wrath*

Though public awareness of migrant suffering was growing, it became ubiquitous with the publication of *The Grapes of Wrath* in the spring of 1939. Although Denning asserts that the "racial populism" of *The Harvest Gypsies* "deeply inflects *The Grapes of Wrath* as well," I would argue that the novel does not simply reproduce the articles' racism as Denning seems to imply. On one level, it is undoubtedly true that the novel is inflected by racism; there are no Mexican or Filipino workers in *Grapes*, and Ma's claim that the Joads descend from soldiers in the American Revolution sounds—when read with *The Harvest Gypsies*—like a reference to their Anglo-Saxon pioneer blood. The first point is arguably the more egregious one: there could be no sustainable, whites-only solution to the problem of exploitation; wage competition between racial groups would only play into the growers' hands. Furthermore, the near erasure of non-whites in the novel meant that much of the militant history of farmworker organizing would be forgotten.

In fact, I would argue that *The Grapes of Wrath* is a call for solidarity from a middle-class novelist to a similar audience. It attempts—not always successfully—to leave behind the frightened condescension of *The Harvest Gypsies* and to reveal a shared humanity, and, more subtly, a shared condition among members of all non-owning classes. Steinbeck's insight—which Denning misses—is that poor migrants and middle-class readers are both workers and ultimately victims of the same social processes, if in different ways. Thus, what was at stake was not merely sympathy, or even respect for other races, but the possibility of a revolutionary understanding of the mode of production. . . .

While I have read the novel as having a radical critique of capitalism and as calling for a socialist solidarity, there are qualifications and counterarguments that could be raised to such a reading. Denning's argument is that the novel is embedded in the same racial nationalism evident in *The Harvest Gypsies*. In one sense, that argument is impossible to refute: *Grapes* mentions non-white workers only briefly while recounting the history of migrant farming before the Okies. Therefore, the existing non-white workers—while at that moment fewer in number than before—are erased. The anticapitalist critique thus exists side-by-side with this erasure—a contradiction that goes unresolved. However, I would argue that the novel otherwise implicitly complicates a simple racial nationalism. Foremost, in contrast with the claims of *The Harvest Gypsies*, *Grapes* shows that the Okies' vaunted Anglo-Saxon racial heritage will not save them. It is only through collective action that they can prevail.

Personal Morality Is Compromised by Corporate Values

Joseph Allegretti

Joseph Allegretti was a practicing lawyer and law school profes-sor for ten years before entering Yale University to obtain a master's degree in divinity. His book The Lawyer's Calling: Christian Faith and Legal Practice *was published in 1996.*

While Steinbeck's setting for The Grapes of Wrath *was the United States of the 1930s, the novel's portrayal of personal and business roles is still relevant today, in the view of Joseph Alle-gretti. The employee's role within the corporation often dimin-ishes a sense of personal responsibility. The person becomes the role, often engaging in conduct that he or she would ordinarily condemn. According to Allegretti, the actions of the tractor men in the novel are a prime example of role morality overriding per-sonal morality. They serve the material priorities and values of the corporation, at the expense of their own sense of right and wrong. In* The Grapes of Wrath, *Allegretti asserts, Steinbeck calls for the transformation of the business world to one in which individuals are not forced to choose between corporate and personal morality. Steinbeck also advocates for employees to transcend the limits of employer-imposed roles and take personal responsibility for their actions.*

John Steinbeck may seem like an unlikely resource for busi-ness ethics in the 21st century. After all, Steinbeck is often characterized as a proletarian writer whose best work dispas-sionately dissected the lives of the uprooted and homeless during the Great Depression. . . . What can *The Grapes of Wrath* contribute to current debates about agri-business and genetically engineered vegetables? Isn't Steinbeck's focus on rural life and itinerant workers hopelessly irrelevant to the contemporary world of insider trading, multinational corporations, and internet commerce?

This view of Steinbeck asks too much and too little of him. It is too much to expect Steinbeck to provide answers to the specific ethical problems that afflict business today. But neither can Sophocles nor Shakespeare provide direct guidance to the businessperson trying to decide whether to misstate corporate earnings, dump toxic substances in a river, or sell an unsafe product. This does not mean that Steinbeck is irrelevant to the world of business and business ethics. . . .

When we experience great works of literature, our life story intersects with the story we are reading. Psychiatrist Robert Coles puts it well: "Novels and stories are renderings of life; they can not only keep us company, but admonish us, point us in new directions, or give us the courage to stay a given course. They can offer us kinsmen, kinswomen, comrades, advisers—offer us other eyes through which we might see, other ears with which we might make soundings." At its best, literature furnishes us with "a moment of recognition, of serious pause, of tough self-scrutiny."

This is how Steinbeck can contribute to business ethics students and to businesspersons seeking moral guidance. As an illustration, let us consider the lessons for business and business ethics from Steinbeck's most famous novel, *The Grapes of Wrath*.

Losing the Person in the Role

Many standard textbooks in business ethics adopt a similar approach to their topic: early in the book, ethical theories such as utilitarianism [the greatest good for the greatest number] and deontology [the study of moral obligations] are explained, and these theories are then employed to analyze real and hypothetical case studies about the environment, consumer safety, job discrimination, and the like. The focus is on knowing and applying philosophical principles to make decisions. Little attention is paid to the *contexts* in which decisions are made. Few of the major textbooks, for example, analyze in any detail the extent to which an employee's *role* within a corporation affects her approach to ethical issues. . . .

Roles, . . . , can diminish an employee's sense of personal responsibility for her actions. As a result, she may find herself engaging in conduct that she would ordinarily condemn as immoral. When this happens, role morality overrides personal morality.

I know of no more dramatic and forceful presentation of role morality than Steinbeck's discussion of the tractor men in chapter 5 of *The Grapes of Wrath*. Chapter 5 is one of the interchapters in which Steinbeck "universalizes" his story by expanding his narrative eye beyond the Joad family. The chapter is divided into three parts. In the first part, the owners and their agents come onto the dry and unproductive land being farmed by their sharecropping tenants. They bring terrible news: the tenants and their families must pack up and leave immediately. In the second part, the owners send in tractors to plow up the lands, destroy the fences and buildings that sit there, and drive off the tenants. In the final part, one of the tenant farmers confronts a tractor driver and the driver defends his actions. The several sections of chapter 5 are linked by their focus on the way moral responsibility is diffused and diluted by the roles people play.

Owners and Agents Bring News

In the first part of chapter 5, the owners or their agents come onto the land. Steinbeck writes, "Some of the owner men were kind because they hated what they had to do, and some of them were angry because they hated to be cruel, and some of them were cold because they had long ago found out that one could not be an owner unless one were cold. And all of them were caught in something larger than themselves." The personalities of the owners change—some become kind, some become cruel—as they wrestle with nagging moral doubts about their actions. They subdue these doubts by convincing themselves that they have no choice but to dispossess their tenants. It's not their fault—it's the bank, it's the company, that is responsible. This bank, this company, is something inhuman, amoral, a machine. More than that, the owners call it a "monster" that needs money like humans need air. Banks and companies "don't breathe air, don't eat side-meat. They breathe profits; they eat the interest on money. If they don't get it, they die the way you die without air, without side-meat. It's a sad thing, but it is so. It is just so."

The tenant farmers plead for more time, just one more year, but to no avail. The sharecropping system is dead and finished, say the owners. The banks will hire a few men to grow cotton, pay them a wage, and take the crop for as long as they can until they kill off the land. The tenant farmers must leave immediately. And as the farmers plead their case, the owners do little more than repeat a litany of denial:

It's not us, it's the bank. . . .

We're sorry. It's not us. It's the monster. The bank isn't like a man. . . .

The bank is something more than men, I tell you. It's the monster. Men made it, but they can't control it. . . .

No. The bank, the monster owns it. You'll have to go. . . .

We're sorry, said the owner men. The bank, the fifty-thousand-acre owner can't be responsible.

The Tractor Men Arrive

This abdication of personal moral responsibility is addressed directly in the second portion of chapter 5 when the tractor men arrive to plow under the fields and evict the tenant farmers. The men on the tractors have relinquished their humanity and become things, machines, objects of destruction. Their very appearance reveals their loss of humanity: "The man sitting in the iron seat did not look like a man; gloved, goggled, rubber dust mask over nose and mouth, he was a part of the monster, a robot in the seat." Goggled and muzzled, the tractor men cannot feel or smell the land and have lost all connection to it: "If a seed dropped did not germinate, it was nothing. If the young thrusting plant withered in drought or drowned in a flood of rain, it was no more to the driver than to the tractor." Scholars sometimes bemoan the loss of personal responsibility that comes from being a small cog in a great machine, but few writers have captured this loss of moral agency so acutely and vividly.

Farmer and Tractor Man

In the final part of chapter 5, Steinbeck recounts a conversation between one of the tractor men and a tenant farmer:

"Why, you're Joe Davis's boy!"

"Sure," the driver said.

"Well, what you doing this kind of work for—against your own people?"

"Three dollars a day. I got damn sick of creeping for my dinner—and not getting it. I got a wife and kids. We got to eat. Three dollars a day, and it comes every day."

"That's right," the tenant said. "But for your three dollars a day fifteen or twenty families can't eat at all. Nearly a hundred people have to go out and wander on the roads for your three dollars a day. Is that right?"

And the driver said, "Can't think of that. Got to think of my own kids. Three dollars a day, and it comes every day. Times are changing, mister, don't you know? Can't make a living on the land unless you got two, five, ten thousand acres and a tractor. . . . You try to get three dollars a day someplace. That's the only way."

Joe Davis's son is not evil-spirited or mean, but he has a job to do, a role to play. In the language of philosopher Richard Wasserstrom, the tractor man sees himself as an "amoral technician" whose only duty is to do what his job requires, no questions asked. When he is at home he may be kind and compassionate, but when he is at work he embraces the "dog-eat-dog" mentality and the "I'm-only-following-the-rules" excuse.

In desperation a tenant farmer threatens to kill the tractor driver. But what good will that do? As the driver points out, "And look—suppose you kill me? They'll just hang you, but long before you're hung there'll be another guy on the tractor, and he'll bump the house down. You're not killing the right guy." The frustrated farmer asks, "Who gave you orders? I'll go after him. He's the one to kill." But that won't work either. The tractor men get their orders from the bank, the bank gets its orders from a president and board of directors, the directors get their orders from someone or something back East. The chain of command extends back indefinitely, with the bewildered driver himself concluding, "I don't know. Maybe there's nobody to shoot. Maybe the thing isn't men at all."

Only the "system" seems responsible. But who, then, is really responsible? Is anyone responsible at all? As [author] Thomas Carson explains:

The farmer is adamantly defending the view that individuals or groups of individuals are always responsible for corporate actions. . . . He contends that some individual human being (or some group of human beings) is responsible for evicting him from his home and he is determined to kill whoever it is that is responsible. The bulldozer driver questions whether there is any individual person (or group of persons) who is responsible for evicting the farmer. He rejects various attempts by the farmer to hold particular individuals responsible for his eviction.

Organizations Have Their Own Set of Values

Steinbeck is doing more in this passage than presenting competing sides in a moral debate. The debate between the farmer and the driver raises an important point for business and one too often overlooked by business ethicists—*organizations have a life of their own.* Individuals make up a company, but a company has its own culture, values, and morality. This corporate ethos encourages certain behavior and discourages other behavior. The corporate culture at Enron, for example, focused on obtaining short-term profits and driving up the stock price. There was a "win-at-all-costs" mentality. Employees who raised doubts about the way deals were structured and recorded were punished, while those who went along with the corporate culture were lavishly rewarded. The corporate ethos, then, can act like a cloak to obscure the moral responsibility of the individuals who make up the company. . . . Steinbeck's story of the tractor men shows how membership in a group can create a kind of moral blindness that ultimately leads to a loss of moral agency. . . .

Steinbeck's portrayal of the tractor men is as contemporary as this morning's business headlines. The tractor men are no different from the corporate executive who breaks the law because her boss tells her to, the stockbroker who makes a killing by illegal insider trading because everyone else is doing it, the accountant who shreds documents to protect a client, or the research scientist who fudges data because further tests could cost the company profits. In each case, the role has gobbled up the person.

Transcending Roles and Role Morality

Chapter 5 ends with a tenant farmer and his family watching helplessly as a tractor man demolishes their house. The message seems to be that ordinary men and women are powerless against the forces of mechanization, bureaucratization, and corporate mentality. Our last image of the tractor man reminds us of the price he has paid for his "three dollars a day": "And the driver was goggled and a rubber mask covered his nose and mouth." He has traded his humanity for a paycheck.

The real question is not whether the tractor men (or the banks, for that matter) are acting ethically or unethically by dispossessing the tenant farmers. The real question is whether they even recognize that their actions raise a moral issue. Steinbeck raises the question whether it is possible to move from moral blindness to moral awareness. Is there any way to escape the moral tunnel vision that too often accompanies a role? Most business ethicists are silent on this point. . . .

Role Becomes a "Mask"

A role can be transformed into a "mask" that denies one's essential humanity and moral responsibility, for [as I wrote in a 1993 essay] "The risk of wearing a mask is that the I, the self behind the mask, will be lost." In order to guard against the loss of the self, workers need to cultivate a healthy detachment from their roles. The need to remember that they are more than the roles they play—they retain [as author Michael Hardiman wrote] "duties that are independent of one's role, duties that apply to people generally."

Employers, of course, have an important part to play here. A company can either encourage or discourage an exaggerated sense of role identification on the part of its workers. A company that is truly committed to moral reflection can take several concrete steps—for example, it can provide ethics training for workers and supervisors, adopt a clear ethics policy, establish procedures for employees to raise ethical questions and report ethical lapses, incorporate ethics into reward systems for workers and managers, and so on.

Transforming the Business World

Here again Steinbeck has something valuable to contribute to business ethics. His concern, however, is not with the corporation's efforts to create an ethical climate—it is both broader and narrower than that. Steinbeck's response to the problem of excessive role identification and the loss of personal responsibility proceeds at two levels—the macro level of society and the micro level of the individual worker. At the macro level, Steinbeck is calling for the transformation of the business world and economy. If all persons could find good paying and meaningful work in organizations that respect and reward moral conduct, then employees would no longer feel a need to hide behind their roles to avoid responsibility for their actions. *The Grapes of Wrath* can be read as an appeal for the creation of a more just and compassionate economy—an economy where the son of Joe Davis will not have to choose between dispossessing his neighbors or earning enough to feed his children.

Employees Can Reject Roles

Steinbeck also suggests a second way to counter the morally deadening effects of a role. This way is more personal, less dramatic, but perhaps equally radical. Employees can begin to see themselves and what they do in a new light, a transformation beautifully described in chapter 26 of *The Grapes of Wrath*. In this chapter the Joads are picking peaches and living at a company-owned camp. When Ma goes to buy food at the company store, she encounters a clerk who seems to epitomize a narrow role morality. Even his physical description reveals his cramped moral sensibilities: he is a "tiny man," "completely bald," whose nose is "long and thin, and curved like a bird's beak." When Ma notes how expensive his prices are compared to the costs in town, the clerk offers no sympathy. His tone is sharp and condescending. Finally, Ma confronts him directly:

"You own this here store?"

"No, I jus' work here."

"Any reason you got to make fun? That help you any?" She regarded her shiny wrinkled hands. The little man was silent. "Who owns this here store?"

"Hooper Ranches, Incorporated, ma'am."

"An' they set the prices?"

"Yes, ma'am."

She looked up, smiling a little. "Ever'body comes in talks like me, is mad?"

He hesitated for a moment. "Yes, ma'am."

"An' that's why you make fun?"

"What cha mean?"

"Doin' a dirty thing like this. Shames ya, don't it? Got to act flip, huh?" Her voice was gentle. The clerk watched her, fascinated. He didn't answer.

The clerk grows silent as if waiting for something to happen. When Ma asks him how he came to take this job, his reply echoes the voice of the tractor man in chapter 5: "'A fella got to eat,' he began; and then, belligerently, 'A fella got a right to eat.'" Ma's response cuts like a knife: "What fella?" she asks. The clerk's first response states a biological fact ("A fella got to eat"), but his second response makes a moral claim ("A fella got a right to eat"). Ma accepts this moral claim but widens it. By asking "What fella?" she is really proclaiming "All people." The clerk has a moral right to eat, but so does Ma, her family, and all human beings. The clerk's snide and sarcastic exterior falls away as Ma's criticism strikes home. He drops his belittling tone and begins to address Ma with respect, acknowledging their common humanity—they are both human beings struggling to survive in a hostile world.

As Ma gets ready to leave with her meager purchases, she remembers that she has no sugar for coffee. Her family is out working in the fields; surely she can have the sugar now and pay him the ten cents when they finish for the day. At first the clerk refuses. "The little man looked away—took his eyes as far from Ma as he could. 'I can't do it,' he said softly. 'That's the rule. I can't. I'd get in trouble. I'd get canned.'" Once again he tries to escape into his role. But now a surprising thing happens. The clerk looks at Ma and "then his face lost its fear." He takes ten cents from his own pocket and pays for the sugar. "'There you are,' he said. 'Now it's all right. You bring in your slip an' I'll get my dime back.'"

For Ma, the lesson of this encounter is, "If you're in trouble or hurt or need—go to poor people. They're the only ones that'll help—the only ones." But there is another lesson here, one equally important. Trapped by the confines of his role, worried about his own livelihood, the store clerk is like the tractor man from chapter 5—his moral universe is limited to his own self-interest. In chapter 5, however, the characters are all abstract and impersonal; there are owners, banks, tractor men, and tenant farmers. Here in chapter 26 the clerk comes face to face with Ma Joad, a real woman of character, commitment, and fierce love. He is no longer a faceless clerk dealing with a nameless customer. He is a human being encountering another human being. In that one-to-one relationship, he changes.

Parallel Transformations

The transformation of the store clerk is the small-scale parallel of the transformation of the Joad family. As *The Grapes of Wrath* opens, the Joads care for little beyond the welfare of their own family. But as they journey westward and their nuclear family begins to disintegrate, they slowly begin to undergo a transformation of consciousness. As [critic] Louis Owens explains:

> From the outset of the migration to California . . . the family begins to change as the nuclear family that Ma holds so dear begins to fragment and the Joads begin to become part of a larger "organization of the unconsciousness." The first step in this gradual change is the family's inclusion of Casy in the council and on the journey. The final steps are Tom's dedication of his life to all men and Rose of Sharon's breast-feeding of the starving stranger. Between these two ends, Steinbeck makes it clear that the Joads have become part of something much larger than themselves.

In the same way, it is the personal encounter with another suffering human being that empowers the clerk to move beyond the limits of his role. Empathy liberates him—he now realizes that he is part of something larger than himself.

Acknowledging Common Humanity

Steinbeck's lesson for business ethics is simple but profound. Roles can restrict our moral universe. They can function as moral blinders. But roles depend for their power upon the willingness of an employee to see herself in the third person: as a store clerk, a banker, a lawyer, or an accountant. When we see ourselves in the third person, we ask, "What does my job demand of me? What is a clerk, banker, lawyer, or accountant supposed to do?" Our role provides the answer—do what the role expects of you, whether the behavior conforms or conflicts with your own values. But as soon as a store clerk, or any worker, begins to relate to others not as a worker but as a human being, the demands of our common humanity eclipse the duties of role. The worker no longer brushes aside moral issues by claiming, "I was only doing my job" or "I had no choice." Instead, the question now becomes: "Who am *I* and what should *I* do?" Asking such a question can transform persons, the companies in which they work, and the culture at large.

At the end of *The Grapes of Wrath*, says Warren French, the Joads' "education is complete; they have transcended familial prejudices. What happens to them now depends upon the ability of the rest of society to learn the lesson that the Joads have learned." In the same way, the store clerk in chapter 26 has learned the lessons of empathy and accountability that allow him to transcend his role and take responsibility for his actions. Steinbeck leaves us with a question and a challenge: How can we create and nurture business policies and practices that make such moments of transcendence possible?

Machines of Industrialization Are Impersonal Monsters

Robert J. Griffin and William A. Freedman

Robert J. Griffin taught at Yale University; California State University, Hayward; and City College of San Francisco. William A. Freedman taught at Brooklyn College of the City University of New York and the University of Haifa in Israel.

Machines and animals are two dominant metaphors and motifs throughout The Grapes of Wrath. *In most cases, according to Griffin and Freedman, machines are characterized as monstrous or animalistic, raping the land and destroying the livelihood of the migrants. The machines—tractors, large trucks, and the like—epitomize the large-scale efficiency, facelessness, and inhumanity of the industrializing economy, the authors assert. Conversely, the Okies' makeshift and failing vehicles are a metaphor for the slow disintegration of their lives. The authors point out, however, that Steinbeck concedes that machines are neutral, only a symptom of the exploitation experienced by the migrants. When used wisely, machines have the potential to improve the fortunes of the migrants.*

We should like to concentrate on two pervasive motifs in [*The Grapes of Wrath*] namely, the crucially important motifs of *machines* and *animals* which contribute considerably to structure and thematic content. We may call these two the "dominant motifs," but we must remember that extracting these elements is necessarily an act of oversimplification; it is only through their complex relationships with subsidiary motifs and devices, and with the more straightforward narration and exposition and argumentation, that they provide major

Robert J. Griffin and William A. Freedman, "Machines and Animals: Pervasive Motifs in *The Grapes of Wrath,*" *Journal of English and Germanic Philology*, July 1963, pp. 569–580.

symbols integral to the art and substance of the novel. With this qualification in mind, we may proceed to a consideration of machines and animals as sources of tropes [figures of speech], as signs and underscoring devices, and ultimately as persistent symbols.

Machines as Metaphor for Human Actions

Very few of the tropes of the novel—the metaphors, similes, and allusions—make use of machinery as such. "Tractored out" is of course a prominent figure of speech repeated several times to express the Okies' plight in being forced from their plots of land by the mechanical monstrosity of industrialized farming ("tractored off" also appears a couple of times). But otherwise about the only instance of a metaphorical use of machinery is a single simile late in the novel: the weary men trying to build a bank of earth to hold back the flood "worked jerkily, like machines." There are a good many metaphors applied to mechanical apparatuses—that is, tropes in which machinery is characterized by some non-mechanical phenomenon as the vehicle of the metaphor. Generally this metaphorical characterization of machines emphasizes animalism, or the bestial side of human affairs, as the seeders are said to rape the land. Fundamentally these metaphors appear designed to contribute to a general sense of tragedy or disaster indicated by such secondary motifs as the blood tropes—"the sun was as red as ripe new blood" "the earth was bloody in [the sun's] setting light"—and the frequent recurrence of "cut"—"the sun cut into the shade," "the road was cut with furrows.". . .

It should be noted that the animalistic references to people are not as a rule unfavorable ("randy as a billygoat" is scarcely a pejorative in Steinbeck's lusty lexicon). The few derogatory animal tropes are almost all applied to the exploiters (banks, land companies, profiteers) and not to the exploited (the Joads and other Okies). That these latter must behave like the lower animals is not their fault. Their animalism is the result of the encroachments of the machine economy. Machines, then, are frequently depicted as evil objects: they, "tear in and shove the croppers out" "one man on a tractor can take the place of twelve or fourteen families"; so the Okies must take to the road, seeking a new home, lamenting, "lost my land, a single tractor took my land." Farming has become a mechanized industry, and Steinbeck devotes an entire chapter (nineteen) to the tragic results:

> The tractors which throw men out of work, the belt lines which carry loads, the machines which produce, all were increased; and more and more families scampered on the highways, looking for crumbs from the great holdings, lusting after the land beside the roads. The great owners formed associations for protection and they met to discuss ways to intimidate, to kill, to gas.

The Okies are very aware of the evils brought about by mechanization. Reduced to picking cotton for bare-subsistence wages, they realize that even this source of income may soon go. One asks, "Heard 'bout the new cotton-pickin' machine?"

Machines Epitomize Impersonal New Economy

The Joads find themselves living—trying to live—in an age of machinery. Machines or mechanized devices quite naturally play important roles in the symbolism of the novel. ("Symbolism" is here understood to mean the employment of concrete images—objects and events—to embody or suggest abstract qualities or concepts.) Some machines serve as "interior" symbols; they are, that is, recognized as symbolic by characters in the novel. Still others, largely because of the frequency with which or crucial contexts in which they appear, can be seen by the careful reader to take on symbolic significance. The "huge red transport truck" of chapter two, for example, can be seen as a sort of epitome of the mechanical-industrial economy—the bigness, the newness, the mobility, the massive efficiency, even the inhumanity (*No Riders*) and lack of trust—"a brass padlock stood straight out from the hasp on the big back door." It is a mobile era in which one must accommodate to the mass mechanization in order to survive. Farmers can no longer hope to get by with a team and a wagon. And Steinbeck finds in the used-car business (chapter seven), preying on the need to move out and move quickly, an apt representation for the exploitation of those who have not yet been able to accommodate. "In the towns, on the edges of the towns, in fields, in vacant lots, the used-car yards, the wreckers' yards, the garages with blazoned signs—Used Cars, Good Used Cars, Cheap Transportation." The Joads' makeshift truck aptly represents their predicament—their need to move, their inability to move efficiently or in style, their over-all precariousness: "The engine was noisy, full of little clashings, and the brake rods banged. There was a wooden creaking from the wheels, and a thin jet of steam escaped through a hole in the top of the radiator cap." Steinbeck makes overt the symbolic nature of this truck; when the members of the family meet for their final council before migrating, they meet near the truck. "The house was dead, and the fields were dead; but this truck was the active thing, the living principle." Here, as throughout the novel, the Joads' predicament is a representative instance of the predicaments of thousands. Highway 66 is the "main migrant road" (chapter twelve), and on this "long concrete path" move the dispossessed, the "people in flight": "In the day ancient leaky radiators sent up columns of steam, loose connecting rods hammered and pounded. And the men driving the trucks and the overloaded cars listened apprehensively. How far between towns? It is a terror between towns. If something breaks— well, if something breaks we camp right here while Jim walks to town and gets a part and walks back." Along this route the dispossessed farmers find that they are not alone in their troubles. The independent, small-scale service station operator is being squeezed out of his livelihood just as the farmers have been; Tom tells the poor operator that he too will soon be a part of the vast moving. And the various types of vehicles moving along Route 66 are obvious status symbols. Some have "class an' speed"; these are the insolent chariots of the exploiters. Others are the beat-up, overloaded conveyors of the exploited in search of a better life. The reactions of those who are better-off to the sad vehicles of the Okies are representative of their lack of understanding and sympathy:

"Jesus, I'd hate to start out in a jalopy like that."

"Well, you and me got sense. Them goddamn Okies got no sense and no feeling. They ain't human. A human being wouldn't live like they do. A human being couldn't stand it to be so dirty and miserable. They ain't a hell of a lot better than gorillas."

Okies' Cars Mirror Their Owners' Sad State

The Okies are conscious of vehicles as status symbols and automatically distrust anyone in a better car. When a new Chevrolet pulls into the laborers' camp, the laborers automatically know that it brings trouble. Similarly the condition of the Okies' vehicles provides perfect parallels for their own sad state. As the Joads are trying to move ahead without being able to ascertain exactly where they are headed—even if we got to crawl—so their truck's "dim lights felt along the broad black highway ahead." As the Joads' condition worsens, so naturally does that of their truck (e.g., "the right head light blinked on and off from a bad connection"). In the development of the novel their vehicles are so closely identified with the Okies that a statement of some damage to the vehicles becomes obviously symbolic of other troubles for the owners. When the disastrous rains come, "beside the tents the old cars stood, and water fouled the ignition wires and water fouled the carburetors." The disastrousness of the ensuing flood is

Steinbeck's characters and their real-life counterparts struggled against the machines that threatened their livelihood. William Sumits/Time & Life Pictures/Getty Images.

quite clearly signaled by mention of the "trucks and automobiles deep in the slowly moving water."...

Animal Symbolism

Animals convey symbolic significance throughout the novel. When the Okies are about to set out on what they are aware will be no pleasure jaunt to California—though they scarcely have any idea how dire will be the journey and the life at the end of it—an ominous "shadow of a buzzard slid across the earth, and the family all looked up at the sailing black bird." In the light of the more obvious uses of animals as epitomes or omens, it is easy to see that other references to animals, which might otherwise seem incidental, are intentionally parallel to the actions or troubles of people. Here is a vivid parallel for the plight of the share-cropper, caught in the vast, rapid, mechanized movement of the industrial economy (the great highway is persistently the bearer of symbolic phenomena):

> A jackrabbit got caught in the lights and he bounced along ahead, cruising easily, his great ears flopping with every jump. Now and then he tried to break off the road, but the wall of darkness thrust him back. Far ahead bright headlights appeared and bore down on them. The rabbit hesitated, faltered, then turned and bolted toward the lesser lights of the Dodge. There was a small soft jolt as he went under the wheels. The oncoming car swished by. . . .

We have seen that both machines and animals serve as effective symbolic devices in *The Grapes of Wrath*. Frequently the machine and animal motifs are conjoined to afford a doubly rich imagery or symbolism. Thus the banks are seen as monstrous animals, but *mechanical* monsters: "the banks were machines and masters all at the same time." The men for whom the share-croppers formerly worked disclaim responsibility: "It's the monster. The bank isn't like a man." The tractors that the banks send in are similarly monstrous—"snub-nosed monsters, raising the dust and sticking their snouts into it, straight down into the country, across the country, through fences, through dooryards, in and out of gullies in straight lines." And the man driving the tractor is no longer a man; he is "a part of the monster, a robot in the sea." Their inability to stop these monsters represents the frantic frustration of the dispossessed; Grampa Joad tries to shoot a tractor, and does get one of its headlights, but the monster keeps on moving across their land. The new kind of mechanical farming is contrasted with the old kind of personal contact with the land. The new kind is easy and efficient. "So easy that the wonder goes out of work, so efficient that the wonder goes out of land and the working of it, and with the wonder the deep understanding and the relation."

Machines Are Not Inherently Evil

We have seen that machines are usually instruments or indices of misfortune in Steinbeck's novel. But to assume that machinery is automatically or necessarily bad for Steinbeck would be a serious mistake. Machines are *instruments*, and in the hands of the right people they can be instruments of good fortune. When the turtle tries to cross the highway, one driver tries to smash him, while another swerves to miss him; it depends on who is behind the wheel. Al's relationship with the truck is indicative of the complex problems of accommodating in a machine age. He knows about motors, so he can take care of the truck and put it to good use. He is admitted to a place of responsibility in the family council because of his up-to-date ability. He becomes "the soul of the car." The young people are more in tune with the machines of their times, whereas the older ones are not prepared to accommodate to the exigencies of the industrial economy. . . .

The tractors that shove the croppers off their land are not inherently evil; they are simply the symptoms of unfair exploitation. In one of the interchapters (fourteen) Steinbeck expresses the thought that the machines are in themselves of neutral value:

Is a tractor bad? Is the power that turns the long furrows wrong? If this tractor were ours it would be good—not mine, but ours. If our tractor turned the long furrows of our land, it would be good. Not my land, but ours. We could love that tractor then as we have loved this land when it was ours. But this tractor does two things—it turns the land and turns us off the land. There is little difference between this tractor and a tank. The people are driven, intimidated, hurt by both.

Machinery, like the science and technology that can develop bigger and better crops is not enough for progress; there must be human understanding and cooperation. The Okies—through a fault not really their own—have been unable to adjust to the machinery of industrialization. Toward the very last of the novel Ma pleads with Al not to desert the family, because he is the only one left qualified to handle the truck that has become so necessary a part of their lives. As the flood creeps up about the Joads, the truck is inundated, put out of action. But the novel ends on a hopeful note of human sharing, and we may surmise that the Okies (or at least their children) can eventually assimilate themselves into a machine-oriented society.

Biblical Parallels Emphasize the Spiritual Aspect of the Joads' Journey

Joseph Fontenrose

Joseph Fontenrose (1903–1986) was a professor of Classics at the University of California–Berkeley, where he spent most of his career. He was interested in Greek religion and mythology. He was also considered an expert on Steinbeck and wrote on the mythology in Steinbeck's work.

According to Joseph Fontenrose, the very title of the novel, The Grapes of Wrath, *suggests a biblical allegory. The novel's three basic divisions—drought, travel to California, and settlement in a new land—replicate the mythical model of the Hebrews' exodus from Egypt to a "land of milk and honey." In Fontenrose's view, the migrants are the spiritually driven chosen people; the corporations and landowners are the idol-worshipping Pharaoh and the Egyptian oppressors. Further, the Joad family and Casy can be viewed as representations of biblical figures including Moses and Jesus. In this context, Fonterose asserts, the story becomes one of spiritual struggle, an epic that transcends the plight of the migrants to communicate a more universal message.*

The title [of *The Grapes of Wrath*] suggests a Biblical parallel, since [poet] Julia Ward Howe's "vintage where the grapes of wrath are stored" obviously alludes to Revelation 14:19, "the great winepress of the wrath of God." [Literary critic] Peter Lisca has accurately pointed to the principal mythical model: the exodus of the Hebrews from Egypt to Canaan. He shows that the novel's three well-marked divisions—drought (Chapters 1–10), journey (11–18), and so-

Joseph Fontenrose, "The Grapes of Wrath," *John Steinbeck: An Introduction and Interpretation*, New York: Barnes & Noble, 1963, pp. 67–83.

journ in California (19–30)—correspond to oppression in Egypt, exodus, and settlement in Canaan: the drought and erosion are the plagues of Egypt; the banks and land companies are Pharaoh and the Egyptian oppressors; California is Canaan, a land flowing with milk and honey; and the Californians, like the Canaanites, are hostile to the immigrants. Lisca also indicates several specific parallels: the symbolism of grapes to indicate either abundance (Numbers 13:23) or wrath and vengeance (Deuteronomy 32:32); the migrants are "the people," and Ma Joad's words, "we're the people—we go on," suggest a chosen people; in the roadside camps the migrants, like the Hebrews, formulated codes of laws to govern themselves; finally, among the willows by a stream John Joad set Rose of Sharon's stillborn child afloat in an apple box, as the infant Moses was placed in a basket among flags in the river.

Parallels with the Exodus

There are other parallels that Lisca does not mention. The name *Joad*, I am sure, is meant to suggest *Judah*. The Joads had lived in Oklahoma peacefully since the first settlement, as the Hebrews had lived in Egypt since Joseph's time. But "there arose up a new king over Egypt, which knew not Joseph" (Exodus 1:8); and the monster, representing a changed economic order, and quite as hard-hearted as Pharaoh, knew not the Joads and their kin. In Oklahoma the dust filtered into every house and settled on everything, as in one of the Egyptian plagues the dust became lice which settled on man and beast (Exodus 8:17); plants were covered, as the locusts devoured every green thing in Egypt (Exodus 10:15); the dust ruined the corn, as hail ruined the Egyptians' flax and barley (Exodus 9:31); and it made the night as black as the plague of darkness in Egypt (Exodus 10:22 f.). On the eve of departure the Joads slaughtered two pigs, more likely victims in Oklahoma than the lambs sacrificed by the Hebrews on Passover (Exodus 12). But whereas the Hebrews despoiled the Egyptians of jewels before leaving (Exodus 12:35 f.), the Joads and other Okies were despoiled of goods and money by sharp businessmen in the land that they left.

On the journey the Joads crossed the Colorado (Red) River (Steinbeck does not mention their crossing the North Fork of the Red River on Highway 66, although he refers several times to the red country of Oklahoma) and the desert. Grampa and Granma Joad, like the elder Israelites, died on the way. Connie Rivers complained about the conditions into which the Joads had led him, and finally deserted them: the Hebrews continually murmured against their leaders on the ground that they were worse off in the desert than in Egypt, and Korah rebelled (Numbers 16). The migrants' fried dough was the unleavened bread of the Israelites, and both peoples longed for meat. The laws of the roadside camp, like the Mosaic law, forbade murder, theft, adultery, rape, and seduction; and they too included rules of sanitation, privacy, and hospitality. In the camps "a man might have a willing girl if he stayed with her, if he fathered her children and protected them," as in Exodus 22:16. "And if a man entice a maid that is not betrothed, and lie with her, he shall surely endow her to be his wife." The migrant lawbreaker was banished from all camps; the Hebrew lawbreaker was either banished or stoned. Steinbeck's repeated "It is unlawful" echoes the "Thou shalt not" of the Decalogue.

Okies as the Locusts of Their Day

On the road west, the Joads met men who were going back to Oklahoma from California. These men reported that although California was a lovely and rich country the residents were hostile to the migrant workers, treated them badly, and paid them so poorly that many migrants starved to death in slack periods. In Numbers 13, scouts whom Moses sent ahead into Canaan came back with the report that "surely it floweth with milk and honey"; nevertheless they made "an evil report of the land which they had searched unto the children of Israel, saying, The land ... is a land that eateth up the inhabitants thereof"; and the natives were giants who looked upon the Hebrews as locusts. Yet the Joads, like Joshua and Caleb [of the Bible], were determined to enter the land. The meanness of California officers at the border, the efforts to turn back indigent migrants, the refusal of cities and towns to let migrant workers enter, except when their labor was needed—in all this we may see the efforts of the Edomites, Moabites, and Amorites to keep the Israelites from entering their countries.

Reaching the Promised Land

In spite of the Canaanites' hostility, the Israelites persisted and took over the promised land. The Book of Joshua ends with victory and conquest. But *The Grapes of Wrath* ends at a low point in the fortunes of the Joads, as if the Exodus story had ended with the Hebrews' defeat at Ai (Joshua 7), when the Canaanites routed an army of 3,000 Israelites and killed a number of them, "wherefore the hearts of the people melted, and became as water. And Joshua rent his clothes, and fell to the earth upon his face. ..." The defeat came upon Israel because Achan had "taken of the accursed thing," that is, from Canaanite spoils which belonged to the Lord he had taken silver, gold, and fine raiment. The migrant Okies met defeat because they had not learned to give up selfish desires for money and possessions: still too many wanted to undercut the pay of fellow-workers and had no feeling of a common cause. But they would accomplish nothing if they did not stand together. The issue is left there, and a happy ending depends on an "if": if the migrants should realize their strength in union. Casy, Tom, and Pa Joad predict a change that is coming, a better time for the people, when they will take matters into their own hands and set them right. And the author foresees doom for the oppressors: "Every little means, every violence, every raid on a Hooverville, every deputy swaggering through a ragged camp put off the day a little and cemented the inevitability of the day." Only future events will tell us how the story ends: it had not ended in 1939.

Inventing the Myth

Perhaps the most striking episodic parallel to Exodus occurs near the end of the novel. When Tom killed the vigilante who struck Casy down and left the region when it looked as if he would be found out, he acted as Moses had done. For "when Moses was grown" he saw an Egyptian beating a Hebrew laborer, and he killed the Egyptian and hid his body in the sand. The next day when he reproved a Hebrew for striking another, the angry offender said, ". . . intendest thou to kill me, as thou killedst the Egyptian?" And Moses, seeing that his deed was known, "fled from the face of Pharaoh, and dwelt in the land of Midian." In the Pentateuch [the first five books of the Hebrew Bible] this happened in Egypt before the Exodus; in *The Grapes of Wrath* it happened in California after the migration. It is another Steinbeck myth inversion. The "house of bondage" is in the new land; in the old land the people had lived in patriarchal contentment until they were forced to leave. It was more like Israel's earlier migration from Palestine to Egypt. Just after reaching California, Tom said to Casy, ". . . this ain't no lan' of milk an' honey like the preachers say. They's a mean thing here." So Moses' task of delivering his people from bondage is just beginning, not ending; it is now that he strikes the first blow. The migrants have gained nothing by merely exchanging one land for another; they must still deal with the "mean thing."

Hence a stillborn child is set adrift upon a stream at the end of the story, rather than a living child at the beginning. It was a "blue shriveled little mummy." This time the first-born of the oppressed had died; yet it was a sign to the oppressors. John Joad said, "Go down an' tell 'em. Go down in the street an' rot an' tell 'em that way. That's the way you can talk." What message? It is given in Chapter Twenty-Five: oranges, corn, potatoes, pigs are destroyed to keep prices up, though millions of people need them. "And children dying of pellagra must die because a profit cannot be taken from an orange."

Tom Joad as the New Moses

Tom Joad becomes the new Moses who will lead the oppressed people, succeeding Jim Casy, who had found One Big Soul in the hills, as Moses had found the Lord on Mount Horeb. As a teacher of a social gospel Casy is more like Jesus than like Moses, and nearly as many echoes of the New Testament as of the Old are heard in *The Grapes of Wrath*. Peter Lisca and [literary critic] Martin Shockley have listed several parallels between the Joad story and the gospel story. Jim Casy's initials are JC, and he retired to the wilderness to find spiritual truth ("I been in the hills . . . like Jesus went into the wilderness . . .") and came forth to teach a new doctrine of love and good works. One of the vigilantes who attacked him pointed him out with the words, "That's him. That shiny bastard"; and just before the mortal blow struck him Casy said, "You don' know what you're a-doin.'" And Casy sacrificed himself for others when he surrendered himself as the man who had struck a deputy at Hooverville. Two Joads were named Thomas, and one became Casy's disciple, who would carry on his teaching. Tom told his mother, "I'm talkin' like Casy," after saying that he would be present everywhere, though unseen, "If Casy knowed," echoing Jesus' words, "Lo, I am with you always. . . ." Lisca and Shockley have also perceived the Eucharist in Rose of Sharon's final act, when she gave her nourishment (the body and blood) to save the life of a starving man.

Twelve Disciples and a Judas

The correspondences between the gospel story and Steinbeck's novel go still deeper than these critics have indicated. Thirteen persons started west, Casy and twelve Joads, who, as we have seen, also represent Judea (Judah) whom Jesus came to teach.

95

Not only were two Joads named Thomas, but another was John; Casy's name was James, brother and disciple of Jesus. One of the twelve, Connie Rivers, was not really a Joad; he is Judas, for not only did he desert the Joads selfishly at a critical moment, but just before he did so he told his wife that he would have done better to stay home "an' study 'bout tractors. Three dollars a day they get, an' pick up extra money, too." The tractor driver of Chapter Five got three dollars a day, and the extra money was a couple of dollars for "[caving] the house in a little." Three dollars are thirty pieces of silver. . . . We should notice too the crowing of roosters on the night when Casy was killed—the only passage, I believe, where this is mentioned—and this at a time when the Joads had to deny Tom.

Casy as Jesus Figure

Casy taught as one with authority: "the sperit" was strong in him. His gospel coincided in certain respects with Jesus' doctrine: love for all men, sympathy for the poor and oppressed, realization of the gospel in active ministry, subordination of formal observances to men's real needs and of property to humanity, and toleration of men's weaknesses and sensual desires. When Casy said, "An' I wouldn' pray for a ol' fella that's dead. He's awright," he was saying in Okie speech, "Let the dead bury their dead" (Luke 9:60).

Casy's doctrine, however, went beyond Christ's. He had rejected the Christianity which he once preached, much as Jesus, starting out as John the Baptist's disciple, abandoned and transformed John's teachings. In *The Grapes of Wrath* John Joad, Tom's uncle, represents John the Baptist, who had practiced asceticism and emphasized remission of sins. John Joad, of course, has almost no literal resemblance to John the Baptist; but he did live a lonely, comfortless life in a spiritual desert, and he was guilt-ridden, obsessed with sin. He was a pious man, a Baptist in denomination; and we hear about his baptism "over to Polk's place. Why, he got to plungin' an' jumpin'. Jumped over a feeny bush as big as a piana. Over he'd jump, an' back he'd jump, howlin' like a dog-wolf in moon time." John, trying to atone for his "sins," was good to children, and they "thought he was Jesus Christ Awmighty." He was, however, the forerunner: for one greater than he had come. When Casy gave himself up to the officers to save Tom, then John realized how unworthy he was beside Casy: "He done her so easy. Jus' stepped up there an' says, 'I done her.'"

It is John Joad's Christianity that Casy rejected. After worrying about his sexual backslidings, Casy came to the conclusion that

> "Maybe it ain't a sin. Maybe it's just the way folks is. . . . There ain't no sin and there ain't no virtue. There's just stuff people do. It's all part of the same thing. And some of the things folks do is nice, and some ain't nice, but that's as far as any man got a right to say."

His doctrine of sin led to his positive doctrine of love: ". . . 'maybe it's all men an' all women we love; maybe that's the Holy Sperit—the human sperit—the whole shebang. Maybe all men got one big soul ever'body's a part of,'" And so he arrived at the doctrine of the Oversoul. "All that lives is holy," he said, and this meant that he should be with other men: "a wilderness ain't no good, 'cause his little piece of a soul wasn't no good 'less it was with the rest, an' was whole." In a California jail his doctrine took complete shape as a social gospel, and Casy's ministry became the organizing of farm workers into unions.

In colloquial language Casy and Tom express the book's doctrine: that not only is each social unit—family, corporation, union, State—a single organism, but so is mankind as a whole, embracing all the rest. . . . The large tracts of uncultivated land that landless farmers could work, and the prophecies that the absentee owners, grown soft, will lose those lands to the dispossessed, strong in adversity and in union, recall the parable of the vineyard: the wicked husbandmen will be destroyed and the vineyard let to other husbandmen who will produce as they should (Matthew 23:33–41). Such owners are like the Scribes and Pharisees, who do not go into the kingdom of heaven themselves, and refuse to let anyone else go in (Matthew 23:13); instead they bind heavy burdens on men's shoulders (Matthew 23:4). Finally, the concluding theme, that family interests must be subordinate to the common welfare, that all individual souls are part of one great soul, corresponds to Jesus' rejection of family ties for the kingdom of heaven's sake: "For whosoever shall do the will of my Father which is in heaven, the same is my brother, and sister, and mother" (Mathew 12:50).

Tom Joad as Disciple and Christ Figure

Tom, Casy's disciple, is a Christ figure, too. He seems at first just another Okie, a man quick to wrath who had killed another man in a brawl at a dance, often rough of speech, and not always kind to others. But we gradually become aware that he is different from his kinsmen. His mother said to him, "I knowed from the time you was a little fella.... Ever'thing you do is more'n you. When they sent you up to prison I knowed it. You're spoke for." In prison he had received a Christmas card from his grandmother, and on it was the verse "Jesus meek and Jesus mild"; thereafter his cell-block mates called him Jesus Meek. The Messianic succession was complete when Tom said farewell to his mother, announcing his intention of taking up Casy's work and trying to induce "our people ... [to] work together for our own thing," to take over all "the good rich lan' layin' fallow" ("he hath anointed me to preach the gospel to the poor.... to set at liberty them that are bruised": Luke 4:18, quoting Isaiah). Though he would vanish from his parents' sight and they would not know where he was, yet, if Casy was right, if a man has no soul of his own, but only a fragment of the one big soul,

"Then it don't matter. Then I'll be all aroun' in the dark. I'll be ever'where—wherever you look. Wherever they's a fight so hungry people can eat, I'll be there. Wherever they's a cop beatin' up a guy, I'll be there. If Casy knowed, why, I'll be in the way guys yell when they're mad an'—I'll be in the way kids laugh when they're hungry an' they know supper's ready. An' when our folks eat at the stuff they raise an' live in the houses they build—why, I'll be there."

It is not only "Lo, I am with you always" but also "where two or three are gathered together . . . there am I in the midst of them," and it is identity with the hungry, thirsty, sick, naked, and imprisoned, as expressed in Matthew 25:35–45. This means also no hate even for the wrongdoers: "The other side is made of men" too, as Doc Burton said in [Steinbeck's] *In Dubious Battle*. When Tom Joad reproved the one-eyed man who reviled his employer, he was in effect saying, "And why beholdest thou the mote that is in thy brother's eye, but considerest not the beam that is in thine own eye?" (Matthew 7:3). . . .

In no Steinbeck novel do the biological and mythical strands fit so neatly together as in *The Grapes Wrath*. The Oklahoma land company is at once monster, Leviathan, and Pharaoh oppressing the tenant farmers, who are equally monster's prey and Israelites. The California land companies are Canaanites, Pharisees, Roman government, and the dominant organism of an ecological community. The family organisms are forced to join together into a larger collective organism; the Hebrews' migration and sufferings weld them into a united nation; the poor and oppressed receive a Messiah who teaches them unity in the Oversoul. The Joads are equally a family unit, the twelve tribes of Israel, and the twelve disciples. Casy and Tom are both Moses and Jesus as leaders of the people and guiding organs in the new collective organism. Each theme—organismic, ecological, mythical; and each phase of the mythical: Exodus. Messiah, Leviathan, ritual sequence—builds up to a single conclusion: the unity of all mankind.

Oakies as Oppressed Israelites

To liken the Okies to the Israelites—this too may seem incongruous. Yet the parallel is really close. The oppressed laborers in Egypt were as much despised by their masters as the migrant workers in California. Moses was certainly a labor agitator, and Jesus appealed to the poor and lowly and called rude fishermen and tax-gatherers to his company. Again the mythical structure imparts a cosmic meaning to the tale. These contemporary events, says Steinbeck, are as portentous for the future as was the Hebrews' migration from Egypt, and for the same reasons.

The myth is accompanied by symbolic images. As the title would lead us to expect, the imagery of grapes, vineyards, and vintage is abundant. As Lisca has pointed out, the grapes mean abundance at first and then bitterness, which turns to wrath as abundant harvests are deliberately destroyed: "In the souls of the people the grapes of wrath are filling and growing heavy, growing heavy for the vintage." The turtle of the early chapters that persistently kept to his south-westward course has been noticed by nearly every reviewer and critic who has discussed *The Grapes of Wrath*. The snakes in this novel have received less attention. After their first view of the fertile California valley from Tehachapi, the Joads went down the road into it, and on the way down they ran over a rattlesnake (Tom was driving), which the wheel broke and left squirming in the road. This is an omen which betokens fulfilment of the behest spoken in the "Battle Hymn of the Republic": "Let the Hero, born of woman, crush the serpent with his heel." The snake represents the agricultural system of California, which the immigrants are destined to crush. Later Al Joad deliberately ran over a gopher snake; when Tom reproved him, Al gaily said, "I hate 'em . . . Hate all kinds." The Okies do not yet know who their friends are.

Steinbeck left the conclusion of his story to events. How did it turn out? On September 1, 1939, fewer than five months after *The Grapes of Wrath* was published, Hitler invaded Poland and began the war which interrupted the course of events that Steinbeck foresaw. In 1940 America began to prepare for war and was in it before the end of 1941. This meant an end of unemployment. The Okies and Arkies came to work in the shipyards of San Francisco and San Pedro bays; they replaced enlisted men in industries and businesses everywhere; and many, of course, were enlisted, too. They found houses to live in, settled down, and remained employed when the war was over. Mexicans and Orientals once more harvested California's crops, and "wet-backs" became a problem. So did *The Grapes of Wrath* never find a conclusion, cut off by the turn of events? Had the owners learned their lesson and improved conditions? Disquieting reports have been coming from the fields: more Americans are now [in 1963] employed in migratory farm labor than a few years ago, pay is low, and conditions are bad. Perhaps the story has not ended yet.

Okies' Transformation from Personal to Political Struggle

Stephen Railton

Stephen Railton is a professor of English at the University of Virginia, where he has taught since 1974. He has published numerous articles on American literature and created two Web-based electronic archives intended to explore the uses of electronic technology for teaching and studying American literature.

In the view of Stephen Railton, the Okies' transformation, interpreted against the laws and rhythms of nature, is one of the underlying themes in The Grapes of Wrath. *The Joads, as are other migrants, are uprooted from their lives as a result of drought and wind. At first, they strive as individual units. But as their journey and suffering unfold, they come to understand that they are part of a larger whole, a universal unity, much like the interrelationships of plants and animals in the natural world. The personal becomes political, asserts Railton, as the sharing of daily life in the camps plants the seeds that transform the migrants into a communal society. As indicated by the book's title, Railton states, the fermenting of change ultimately leads the Joads and other migrant workers to the realization that socialist . . . collective action and helping each other is their only route to overcoming the injustices and hardships they have endured at the hands of the industrialists.*

The Grapes of Wrath is a novel about things that grow—corn, peaches, cotton, and grapes of wrath. From the start Steinbeck identifies his vision of human history with organic, biological processes. A recurrent image is established in the first chapter, when the drought and wind in Oklahoma com-

Stephen Railton, "Pilgrim's Politics: Steinbeck's Art of Conversion," *New Essays on* The Grapes of Wrath, edited by David Wyatt, New York: Cambridge University Press, 1990, pp. 27–46. Reprinted with the permission of Cambridge University Press.

bine to uproot and topple the stalks of corn. In Chapter 29, the last of Steinbeck's wide-angle interchapters, it is the rain and flooding in California that "cut out the roots of cotton-woods and [bring] down the trees." Tragically, even human lives are caught in this pattern of being pulled up from the soil. Farmers are made migrants. Forced to sell and burn all of their pasts that won't fit onto a homemade flatbed truck, they too are uprooted, torn from their identities. Right alongside this pattern, however, Steinbeck establishes a second one: that of seed being carried to new ground, new roots being put down. This image is announced in Chapter 3. The turtle who serves as the agent of movement in that chapter has attracted a lot of commentary from the novel's critics, but Steinbeck's main interest is not in the turtle. Chapter 3 is organized around seeds, all "possessed of the anlage [foundation]." The turtle simply continues on its way, but by involuntarily carrying one "wild oat head" across the road, and accidentally dragging dirt over the "three spearhead seeds" that drop from it and stick in the ground, the mere movement of the turtle becomes part of the process of change and growth.

The Grapes of Wrath is a novel about an old system dying, and a new one beginning to take root. Movement, to Steinbeck, including the movement of history, works like the "West Wind" in [English Romantic poet Percy Bysshe] Shelley's "Ode to the West Wind". It is "Destroyer and preserver" both; it scatters "the leaves dead" and carries forward "The winged seeds." The system that is dying we can call American capitalism, the roots of which had always been the promises of individual opportunity and of private property as the reward for taking risks and working hard. Steinbeck makes it more difficult to name the new system that is emerging from the violent ferment of the old system's decay. It is certainly socialistic, yet a goal of the novel is to suggest that a socialized democracy is as quintessentially American as the individualistic dream it will replace. "Paine, Marx, Jefferson, Lenin" he writes in Chapter 14—this list would confound a historian, but it is meant to reassure the American reader by linking socialism with our own revolutionary tradition. That was one reason for his enthusiasm about the title his wife found for the novel. He wanted the whole of Julia Ward Howe's fighting song ["Battle Hymm of the Republic"] printed as a sort of preface, because, he wrote his editor at Viking,

> The fascist crowd will try to sabotage this book because it is revolutionary. They try to give it the communist angle. However, The Battle Hymn is American and intensely so.... So if both words and music are there the book is keyed into the American scene from the beginning.

An Inevitable Revolution

At the same time, by tying his novel of history to the rhythms and laws of nature, the growth of seeds, the fermenting of grapes, Steinbeck tries to suggest that this coming American revolution is inevitable, organically decreed. The western states sense "the beginning change" with the nervousness of "horses before a thunder storm"; on the road west, separate families "*grew to be* units of the camp."

These repeated biological locutions [expressions] allow the novelist to assume the role of a Darwinian prophet, reading the political future instead of the natural past. Revolution is made to seem as inexorably sure as evolution. The novel is simply recording the process. Yet this quasi-scientific stance, while it helps account for the authority with which Steinbeck's prose tells his story, belies the real engagement of the book. Critics have accused Steinbeck of being wrong, because the drastic social change he apparently predicted never took place. But he knew better than that. If he had himself believed the stance his narrative adopts, he would have written a much less brilliant book, for the novel owes its power to Steinbeck's urgent but painstaking intention to enact the revolution he apparently foresees. Even his assumption of change is part of his strategy for creating it. And Steinbeck knew what he was up against. Despite his desire to make his vision seem "American and intensely so," he undertakes the task of radically redefining the most fundamental values of American society. The novel uproots as much as the forces of either nature or capitalism do, though far more subtly. And, ultimately, there is hardly anything natural about the kind of change—"as in the whole universe only man can change" that Steinbeck is anxious to work. *Supernatural* probably describes it more accurately. Nor is *change* the right word for it, although it's the one Steinbeck regularly uses. *The Grapes of Wrath* is a novel about conversion. . . .

Steinbeck finds much to admire in the Joads and the class of "the people" whom they represent, including the fierce will to survive and keep going which they share with that turtle, but he explicitly makes the capacity for spiritual regeneration the essence of humanity. That humans can redefine the meaning of our lives is what makes us "unlike any other thing organic or inorganic in the universe." Con-version—to turn around, to turn together—is a metaphysical [philosophical] movement. This is the route on which Steinbeck sets the Joads. For, as much as he finds to admire in them, he also knows that before American society can be saved from its sins, "the people" will have to change, too. . . .

Suffering Leads to Spiritual Growth

Steinbeck's antagonist in the novel is not the group of large owners, but rather the idea of ownership itself. It is at the Hooper Ranch that Ma, on the verge of despair, grows most sentimental about the past:

> They was the time when we was on the lan'. They was a boundary to us then. Ol' folks died off, an' little fellas come, an' we was always one thing—we was the fambly—kinda whole and clear. . . .

Yet if owning separates, dispossession becomes the basis for a new unity. If one set of values is being uprooted, that prepares the ground for another to develop. On the one hand, the westward journey of the Joads is a moving record of losses: their home and past, Grampa and Granma's deaths, Noah and Connie's desertions. The sufferings inflicted on the family bear witness not only to their strength of character, but also to the evils of the social and economic status quo. Their hapless pursuit of happiness indicts and exposes the America they move across. . . .

On the other hand, however, the journey of the Joads is also an inward one. And there the same pattern of losses is what converts their movement into a pilgrimage toward the prospect of a new consciousness. As in [John Bunyan's seventeenth-century work] *The Pilgrim's Progress* homelessness and suffering become the occasion of spiritual growth. In several of the interchapters Steinbeck describes this process: "The families, which had been units of which the boundaries were a house at night, a farm by day, changed their boundaries." They expand their boundaries. Having lost their land, the migrants' minds are no longer "bound with acres"; their new lives, their very losses, lead them toward the potentially redemptive discovery of their interrelatedness, their membership in a vastly extended family—the "we." In the novel's main narrative, Steinbeck dramatizes this process; near the very end, Ma sums up the new way she has learned to define her life: "'Use' ta be the fambly was fust. It ain't so now. It's anybody.". . .

Casy Is the Voice of Socialism

It is because Steinbeck's emphasis is on inward experience that Jim Casy, a supernumerary [extra person] as far as most of the book's action is concerned, is central to its plot. Casy's presence is what allows Steinbeck to dramatize his concern with consciousness. At the beginning, Steinbeck gives him a head start on the Joads. They are looking to start over in California; although they have lost their home and land, they still hang on to their belief in the American Dream. Casy, however, is looking to start anew. He has already lost the faith in the Christian values that had given meaning to his life, and is self-consciously questing for a new belief, a new cause to serve. He remains a preacher—long after he has rejected the title, the narrative continues to refer to him as "Reverend Jim Casy" and "the preacher"—but cannot find the Word he should announce. In much the same passivity as the novel's reader, he watches and absorbs the meaning of the Joads' attempt to carry their lives and ambitions westward. His first, indeed his only, decisive action in the narrative itself is precipitated by an act of violence. In the Bakersfield Hooverville, a migrant named Floyd hits a deputy sheriff to avoid being arrested for the "crime" of telling the truth; when the deputy pulls his gun, Tom trips him; when he starts shooting recklessly into the camp, Casy knocks him out—it is worth noting the details because this same sequence will recur at the Hooper Ranch. In describing this action, Steinbeck's prose departs from its usual syntactic straightforwardness to signal its significance: "and then, suddenly, from the group of men, the Reverend Casy stepped." His kicking the deputy in the neck is presented as an instinctual reflex, and his actions, here, and subsequently when he gives himself up to the deputy to save Floyd and Tom, speak a lot louder than any words he uses, but Reverend Casy has at last found a cause to serve.

That cause can be defined as the "group of men" he steps from, but it is also here that Casy disappears from the narrative for 150 pages. In this case Steinbeck refuses to allow his story to get ahead of itself. The exemplary significance of Casy's self-sacrifice is barely registered by the Joads, who still feel they have their own lives to live. And Casy himself cannot conceptualize the meaning of his involuntary action, or the

values of the new faith he commits his life to, until later.
When he reappears at the Hoover Ranch, he tries to explain it
to Tom:

> "Here's me, been a-goin' into the wilderness like Jesus to try
> to find out somepin. Almost got her sometimes, too. But it's
> in the jail house I really got her."

What he got in jail could be called an insight into the
moral logic of socialism: that the greatest evil is human need,
and that the only salvation lies in collective effort. Although
the novel is deliberately vague about how Casy came to be at
the Hooper Ranch, and what his role is in the strike there, we
could see his new identity in strictly political terms: Like the
strike organizers Steinbeck had written about in *In Dubious
Battle*, Casy has committed himself to the cause of Communist revolution. . . .

To the doctrinaire socialist, meaning is found in collective
action. Steinbeck offers his version of that ideal in his descriptions of the government camp at Weedpatch where the Joads
stay for a month after being driven out of the Hooverville.
The camp has a wire fence around it, too, but it only matters
when the forces of capitalism try to destroy the communal
harmony of the camp. The novel presents life in the camp as a
Utopian but practicable antithesis to the selfishness that rules
on both the Joad farm and the Hooper Ranch. In the camp
happiness is pursued by owning things jointly, sharing responsibilities, making decisions by democratically elected commit-
tees. The camp's weekly square dances provide the book's
most attractive image of a communal society: The music be-
longs to no one individual; the dancers obey the calls in uni-
son and joy. It is not an accident that the Growers' Association
and its hired reactionaries try to discredit the camp by dis-
rupting a dance. That episode allows Steinbeck starkly to po-
larize the two worlds, within the camp and without: There's
harmony and expression inside, violence and exploitation
outside. . . .

Spiritual Conversions

What the novel presents as most meaningful are Casy's and Tom's conversions: the purpose and inner peace that each man finds, not in acting with others, but in "feeling" or "seeing" his oneness with all. . . .

The novel's very last scene tries to build a bridge between the realm of spirit, where individuals find their home, and the world of action, where men and women can help each other; it redresses the imbalance of Tom's story, where the emphasis had been almost entirely on faith, by adding to that a doctrine of works. Thematically the novel's last scene is perfect. It is the moment of Rose of Sharon's conversion. Out of the violent loss of her baby (which she has "witnessed" with her whole body) comes a new, self-less sense of self. When she breastfeeds the starving stranger who would otherwise die, a new, boundary-less definition of family is born. Rose of Sharon's act is devoutly socialistic: from each according to ability, to each according to need.

Migrants Were Lured to California by an Unattainable Prize

Jessica B. Teisch

Jessica B. Teisch is managing editor of Bookmarks *magazine and has written hundreds of profiles and book reviews for the publication. She has also written books and articles on subjects ranging from literature to technological, environmental, intellectual, and cultural history.*

In the following viewpoint, Jessica B. Teisch explains that the migrants in The Grapes of Wrath *were lured to California by the promise of riches and fertile land but that those goals were out of their reach for several reasons. They did not know that industrialists and large landowners had already claimed and divided up the desirable land. Further, much of the agricultural success in California was due to an infrastructure and access to water that created a false paradise—and most of the water supply was already spoken for. In addition, the European-style agriculture treated land as a commodity, and private rights, as defined by fences, were paramount. This philosophy was in direct contrast to the traditional Native American respect for, and sharing of, land. Teisch asserts that technology, in the form of tractors and combines, replaced people and loosened the historic bonds that held farmers and their lands together. Ultimately, the Joads had to leave the fraudulent environment and go in search of yet another place to put down roots.*

California's riches did exist, but they dangled beyond the migrants' reach. For Steinbeck's Joads and other environmental refugees, California was [to use a phrase of author

Jessica B. Teisch, "From the Dust Bowl to California: The Beautiful Fraud," *Midwest Quarterly*, vol. 39, winter 1998, pp. 153–172. Copyright © 1998 by *The Midwest Quarterly*, Pittsburgh State University. Reproduced by permission.

Marc Reisner] a "beautiful fraud." Using California as the paradigm for agricultural success after the Dust Bowl, farmers on the Great Plains tapped into underground water and transformed dust into a green paradise. Historical parallels between California and the Plains—settlement in semi-arid lands, federal land policies, land consolidation, new technology, social disintegration—forecast the potential for a calamity as large in scope as the Dust Bowl.

Dust Bowl Migrants Too Late

Environmental events such as the Dust Bowl, which Steinbeck depicts in his fictional *Grapes of Wrath* "remain fixed on people because what we most care about in nature is its meaning for human beings" [writes author William Cronon]. Fiction, or "stories about stories about nature" that act as "our chief moral compass in the world" thus appropriately frame an examination of the human dimension in nature [according to Cronon]. All stories that surround the Dust Bowl's far-reaching consequences, however, begin with the power nature wields over people who fail to include ecological limitations in their calculations.

Steinbeck's Joads left the Southern Plains during the 1930s, not knowing that California had been conquered and divided almost a century earlier. California's extreme fertility juxtaposed with the migrants living amid simultaneous squalor and wealth tells an ironic story that humanizes tragic environmental, social, and political conditions.

In Dust Bowl histories, nature, farmers, governments, and technology all receive parts of the blame. The plight of the Joads largely supports Donald Worster's thesis in *Dust Bowl*, which depicts human defeat in the Southern Plains as the fatal combination of drought and human determination to conquer, divide, and profit from an unyielding land. Worster claims that not only people's plows, but also a "social system, a set of values, a [capitalist] economic order" helped create the Dust Bowl. Yet this social system combined with natural earth processes such as drought "set fundamental limits to what constitutes a plausible narrative," [according to Cronon.]. . .

Majority of Migrants Were Middle-Class Workers

Steinbeck may have imbued his characters with the will to challenge a rigid economic system, yet he tells a monolithic story within the broader scope of westward migration. Like other writers, Steinbeck failed to convey that the majority of migrants were different from his Joads. Most of the 1930s migrants who fled the Southern Plains and moved to California were neither destitute nor the dirt farmers of "popular paradigm" [in the words of author James Gregory]. Representing the land of new beginnings, California had attracted middle class workers with the desire to make a fortune ever since the Gold Rush. Most migrants were not the "illiterate-sounding" characters "close to the soil" like the Joads.

Despite popular perceptions, fewer than 16,000 Dust Bowl refugees moved to California. Many others, especially from areas only peripheral to the most severe wind- and dust-eroded joint corners of Colorado, New Mexico, Kansas, Oklahoma, and Texas, also migrated west. For all its good intentions, *The Grapes of Wrath* solidified some of the unfortunate stereotypes of newcomers; the Joads embody only a small group of nomads wandering helplessly from one difficulty to the next. Only two or three percent of the 50,000 people who migrated from Oklahoma to other states actually came from the western part of the state most affected by dust storms.

Regardless of migratory patterns, inhabitants from the Plains inundated California. In changing the ecology of an arid land comparable to the Great Plains, California succeeded in altering its face into a productive greenbelt during the 1920s reclamation binge. This command over nature suggests that had the Great Plains been engineered in a similar way as California's central desert, the Dust Bowl might have been prevented. . . .

Agricultural Style Conflicted with Native Uses

Despite [John Wesley] Powell's prophetic claim that the West never could be settled in the "yeoman farmer" ideal encouraged by [Thomas] Jefferson, the West, [as explained by author Walter Prescott Webb] "uninhabitable with the methods and implements and instruments of pioneering," was settled. Each group of European settlers not only brought its own customs to America, but also a European-style agriculture based on monoculture and animal power. Domesticated grazing animals required a new system of land management that conflicted with Native Americans' uses and created patterns of land covered with "seemingly endless miles of fences" [as Cronon wrote]. Immigrants also arrived with "belief systems that were hostile to . . . alien forms of knowledge," believing in a nature that was "separate from and subordinate" to them [according to author Jane Smiley]. Dividing land according to individual rather than collective rights "treated members of an ecosystem as isolated and extractable units" [in Cronon's words]. . . .

Steinbeck places the Joads against the backdrop of this land conquest. Tom Joad explains, "it's our land [because] we measured it and broke it up. . . . Even if it's no good, it's still ours. That's what makes it ours—being born on it, working it, dying on it. That makes ownership." The Land Ordinance of 1785, which constructed simple procedures for land distribution, assumed that an organized system could best serve the growing country's needs by placing public land into private hands. Settlement policies such as the Preemption Act, Timber Culture Act, and Desert Land Act encouraged, for the most part, homesteading in a seasonal desert. In the Homestead Act

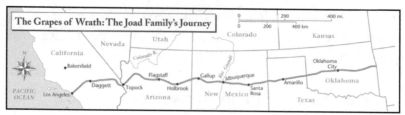

This map traces the Joad family's journey from Oklahoma to California. Reproduced by permission of Gale, a part of Cengage Learning.

of 1864, Congress expected the American West to duplicate the American East. Without irrigation, however, a quarter-section farm in the middle of the Great Plains without water rights was "not a ticket to independence but to starvation" [as author Richard White wrote].

Steinbeck's Joads became tenants under monopolistic and often fraudulent practices that consolidated irrigable tracts of 160 and then eventually 2,560 acres. Powell had stressed that "the right to use water should inhere in the land to be irrigated" to ensure that water rights would not be severed from land rights. Despite this prophetic warning, states west of the one hundredth meridian were subject to the doctrine of prior appropriation. Wealthy landowners bought and concentrated failing farms; the only way to increase output without farm enlargement was to use available land more intensively. . . .

New Landowners Unconnected to the Land

A great irony exists between this massive land consolidation and the farmers. The owners no longer "worked on their farms. They farmed on paper; and they forgot the land, the smell, the feel of it, and remembered only that they owned it, remembered only what they gained and lost by it" [as Steinbeck wrote]. Legal title to land passed to those indifferent to its preservation, determined to reconstruct the landscape into real assets and commodities. Ironically, tenants who maintained a physical connection with the land were the ones expelled from it during the severe droughts in the 1930s.

Technology had a large share in alienating humans from the land. Not until the 1930s, however, when petroleum-driven machines rapidly and permanently displaced animal and human power, did technology exert its power on rural life; new tractors and combines pushed tenants off the land. In her short story "Harvest," Meridel LeSueur condemns this new technology. As a late-nineteenth-century Bohemian woman despairingly watches her husband purchase a tractor, she feels "a flame from the earth, broken off as if the quick of it had taken to his very flesh" consume him. Instead of metal parts, she sees "big knives thrusting back movement even in their stillness" and the "monstrous glint" of the machine.

Steinbeck likewise describes the Joads' fear of the technology that devalued the land and their rural life. When in the 1930s farm owners realized they had to "take cotton quick before the land dies," they replaced people with tractors neither practical nor affordable to farmers on smaller tracts of land. Tractors "came over the roads and into the fields . . . snubnosed monsters, raising the dust and sticking their snouts into it . . . straight across the country." As the Joads went bankrupt, they informed the land company that it was "buying bitterness. Buying a plow to plow your own children under, buying the arms and spirits that might have saved you." . . .

Joads Find California Already Owned by Industry

Steinbeck depicts the recurring greed to own, change, and profit from California:

> Once California belonged to Mexico and its land to Mexicans; and a horde of tattered feverish Americans poured in. And such was their hunger for land that they took the land—stole Sutter's land, Guerrero's land. . . . They put up houses and barns, they turned the earth and planted crops. And these things were possession, and possession was ownership. . . . Then, with time, the squatters were no

longer squatters, but owners; and their children grew up and had children on the land.

The Joads, fleeing a land in which they no longer were an integral part, found in California that "ever'thing is owned. There ain't nothing' left. . . . Purtiest goddamn country you ever seen, but you can't have none of it." As in the Plains states, California's land and water policies and the nature of irrigation agriculture concentrated land ownership. Small farms thrived only where an adequate water supply had been reserved according to prior appropriation. An 1872 California legislative report showed that 122 individuals and companies each owned more then 20,000 acres in California. . . .

Just as small farmers lost their land in the Great Plains, [Steinbeck wrote] "little farmers [in California] who owned no canneries lost their farms, and they were taken by the great owners, the banks, and the companies who also owned the canneries." Farming became an industry by which "the farms grew larger, but there were fewer of them."

Ironically, many small farmers left a monopolized land and fled to one equally inaccessible to the small farmer. As the Joads left the Great Plains and moved to the West, they discovered that California farming had become "industry, and the owners followed Rome, although then, did not know it. They imported slaves, although then, did not call them slaves: Chinese, Japanese, Mexicans, Filipinos." To this scene arrived the Joads, representing the

> dispossessed drawn west—from Kansas, Oklahoma, Texas, New Mexico; from Nevada and Arkansas, families, tribes, dusted out, tractored out. Carloads, caravans, homeless and hungry; twenty thousand and fifty thousand and a hundred thousand and two hundred thousand . . . like ants scurrying for work, for food, and most of all for land.

By 1938, most San Joaquin Valley counties added at least 50 percent to their pre-Depression populations. Over 90 percent of these new immigrants arrived from the Great Plains and Southwest and 32 percent from Oklahoma alone. For the migrant, California was but a "beautiful fraud;" the "fields goaded him, and the company ditches with good water flowing were a goad to him."

In 1935, there were nearly 7 million farms in the United States. By 1974, only 2.3 million remained. During this time, the average farm size increased 183 percent, from 155 acres to 440 acres. Large industrialized farms continued to engulf small farmers. . . .

In one generation, land desperately treasured is lost to a generation that cares primarily for the land's market value. This "imperial and commercial" capitalist ethos, Worster explains, replaced people's connections with the earth. Certainly the Joads live the consequences of treating land as a commodity. . . .

Technology Created a False Eden

As water transformed the Great Plains, California simultaneously developed an $18 billion per year agricultural industry and a migrant culture. Although 65 percent of California receives fewer than twenty inches of rain per year, a luxuriant green veneer camouflages the desert, the result of ingenious technology and labor that captured, channeled, and filtered water all over the state. . . .

Reclamation projects represent only one aspect in the scheme of how technology has altered the landscape and created habitable cities. In the Great Plains, tractors that replaced human labor forced the Joads off the land. The tenant system failed because "one man on a tractor can take the place of twelve or fourteen families." People escaping usurping technology found no welcome mat in California.

In California today a "harvest happens nearly without people" [according to Mark Kramer]. Whereas Steinbeck clearly decries the exploitation of human labor, Mark Kramer, in his short story "The Farmerless Farm," likewise mourns the technological aspect of California's magnificent agricultural revolution. Kramer asserts that "until a few years ago it took a crew of perhaps six hundred laborers to harvest a crop this size." Now hydraulic tractors produce a "dearth of human presence" that reflects the "blandness overlaying a wondrous integration of technology, finances, personnel, and business system." Machine-oriented production depicts both California's agricultural success and its bleak socio-economic conditions. Migrant workers who follow various harvests are needed only at the end of each season, doing what the "electric eye" cannot. This part-time migratory work leaves "a lot of workers on welfare, or whatever they can get, hanging around waiting for the little bit" of work. . . .

Engineered Landscape Cannot Outwit Nature

Not first in a chain of conditions created by early settlers and certainly, not the last, Steinbeck's Joads were forced to leave their fraud. Had they stayed, their farm would be only one among many today that subsists in a region neither a desert nor an eternal agricultural paradise.

The immediate choice of abandoning the land in search of a more fertile one, however, is an equally unattractive option. A haven for thousands of environmental refugees, California was a "beautiful fraud." If California represents the paradigm of successfully engineering the landscape, it also embodies our failure to acknowledge that nature is a system of checks and balances.

The extent to which nature and people influence each other is not in question; instead, this relationship comprises the core of our effort to understand the natural world. Nature, the way it influences people's decisions, and the manner in which people respond to it, tells different stories. Federal land policies, land tenure, and technology, represent various threads in a yarn knotted and twisted by interpretation and individual narratives. Combining these speciously disparate elements enlarges the parallel between the Great Plains and California.

In telling stories in a way that relates to the human condition, Steinbeck and other writers not only help us [as Cronon wrote] "make sense of nature's place in the human past," but also magnify our fractured relationship with the earth. While different stories by their very nature recount one narrative over another, what they hide is equally important in untangling different threads of a story so large in magnitude that it threatens to recur.

Unlike the fictional Joads, who "had gone against a system they did not understand and it had beaten them," we can improve an ingrained land ethic. If we do not venture to change the way we think about our relationship to the land, we will subject ourselves to history's ironies once again.

Steinbeck Exaggerated the Scale of the Okies' Misfortune

Keith Windschuttle

Keith Windschuttle is an author and critic who has written a number of books about Australian history and social issues, including The Fabrication of Aboriginal History.

The Grapes of Wrath, *Steinbeck's portrayal of the Okies and their trials en route to California, was the defining literature of the Great Depression era. However, Keith Windschuttle claims, research on the 1930s has proven many of the novel's descriptions false or greatly exaggerated. Most of the migrants who left Oklahoma in the Depression came from cities and towns, Windschuttle asserts, and they possessed professional and trade skills. They ended up achieving at least a version of the American Dream, with the materialistic gains of a home, secure employment, and a better way of life. According to Windschuttle, the suffering Steinbeck described affected about ninety thousand people, rather than Steinbeck's three hundred thousand. His Marxist-leaning political and social connections likely influenced the portrait he painted, Windschuttle states.*

John Steinbeck performed a rare feat for a writer of fiction. He created a literary portrait that defined an era. His account of the "Okie Exodus" in *The Grapes of Wrath* became the principal story through which America defined the experience of the Great Depression. Even today, one of the enduring images for anyone with even a passing familiarity with the 1930s is that of Steinbeck's fictional characters the Joads, an American farming family uprooted from its home by the twin disasters of dust storms and financial crisis to become refu-

Keith Windschuttle, "Steinbeck's Myth of the Okies," *New Criterion*, vol. 20, June 2002, pp. 24–32. Copyright © 2002 Foundation for Cultural Review. Reproduced by permission of the author.

gees in a hostile world. Not since Dickens's portrayal of the slums of Victorian England has a novelist produced such an enduring definition of his age. . . .

Steinbeck's book was presented at the time as a work of history as well as fiction, and it has been accepted as such ever since. Unfortunately for the reputation of the author, however, there is now an accumulation of sufficient historical, demographic, and climatic data about the 1930s to show that almost everything about the elaborate picture created in the novel is either outright false or exaggerated beyond belief.

For a start, dust storms in the Thirties affected very little of the farming land of Oklahoma. Between 1933 and 1935, severe wind erosion did create a dust bowl in the western half of Kansas, eastern Colorado, and the west Texas/New Mexico border country. While many Oklahoma farms suffered from drought in the mid-1930s, the only dust-affected region in that state was the narrow panhandle in the far west. . . .

[Nothing] like this happened anywhere near where Steinbeck placed the Joad family farm, just outside Sallisaw, Oklahoma, part of the cotton belt in the east of the state, almost on the Arkansas border. In the real dust bowl, it is true that many families packed up and left, but the historian James N. Gregory has pointed out that less than 16,000 people from the dust-affected areas went to California, barely six percent of the total from the southwestern states. . . .

Demographic Errors in *Grapes*

It is true that many people left Oklahoma for California in the 1930s. This was anything but a novel phenomenon, however. People had been doing the same since before World War I, as the southwestern states' economy failed to prosper and as better opportunities were available in other regions. Between 1910 and 1930, 1.3 million people migrated from the southwest to other parts of the United States. In the 1920s, census data show that about 250,000 of them went to California, while in the 1930s this total was about 315,000. The real mass migration of Okies to California actually took place in the 1940s to take advantage of the boom in manufacturing jobs during World War II and its aftermath. In this period, about 630,000 of them went to the west coast. It was not the Depression of the 30s but the economic boom of the 40s that caused an abnormal increase in Okie migration.

Moreover, most of the migrants who did leave Oklahoma in the Depression were not farmers. Most came from cities and towns. The 1940 Census showed that in the period of the supposed great Okie Exodus between 1935 and 1940, only thirty-six percent of southwesterners who migrated to California were from farms. Some fifty percent of these migrants came from urban areas and fitted occupational categories such as professionals, proprietors, clerical/sales, skilled laborers, and semi-skilled/service workers.

Predictably, they had a similar distribution when they joined the Californian workforce. Their favorite destination was Los Angeles, which attracted almost 100,000 Okies between 1935 and 1940, with about a quarter as many going to the cities of San Francisco and San Diego. Of the two major destinations for agricultural workers, the San Joaquin Valley attracted 70,000 and the San Bernardino/Imperial Valley region 20,000 migrants. This fell considerably short of their demographic portrait in *The Grapes of Wrath....*

The Banks Were Not to Blame

Steinbeck blamed the banks for their plight. Rather than allowing small farms and tenant farmers the right to exist, the banks fostered competition, mechanization, land consolidation, and continual expansion. "The bank—the monster has to have profits all the time. It can't wait. When the monster stops growing, it dies. It can't stay one size." He compared this inhuman imperative to the rights of those who worked the land:

> We were born on it, and we got killed on it, died on it. Even
> if it's no good, it's still ours. That's what makes it ours—
> being born on it, working on it, dying on it. That makes
> ownership, not a paper with numbers on it.

> We're sorry [say the owner men]. It's not us. It's the mon-
> ster. The bank isn't like a man.

Ironically, for someone whose politics have been described
by his several biographers as a "typical New Deal Democrat,"
Steinbeck identified the wrong culprit. In two separate studies
of the plight of southern tenant farmers in the 1930s, the historians David Eugene Conrad and Donald H. Grubbs have
blamed not the banks but the agricultural policies of the New
Deal itself. In the early 1930s, some sixty percent of farms in
Oklahoma, Arkansas, and Texas were operated by tenants.
However, during the Depression they found themselves victims of Franklin Roosevelt's 1933 Agricultural Adjustment Act
[AAA], which required landlords to reduce their cotton acre-
age. Fortified by AAA subsidies, the landlords evicted their
tenants and consolidated their holdings. It was government
handouts, not bank demands, that led these landlords to buy
tractors and decrease their reliance on tenant families. By
1940, tenant farmer numbers had declined in the southwest
by twenty-four percent.

Steinbeck Gives a False Impression

In *The Grapes of Wrath*, thirteen members of the Joads' extended family set out in the one vehicle, including grandpar-
ents and grand-children. In two moving scenes, both Grampa
and Granma die en route. Along the way, in-laws and uncles
also abandon them, leaving Ma Joad, who is in her fifties, to
try to keep the rest of the family together. This entourage
would have been demographically unusual. Rather than large
families extending over several generations, the most common
trekkers from the southwest to California were composed of
husband, wife, and children, an average of 4.4 members. Only

twenty percent of households included other relations. Most were young. Of the adults, sixty percent were less than thirty-five years old. They were also better educated than those of the same age group who stayed behind. In other words, they were typical of those who have undertaken migration in every era, whether over the Rockies or across the Atlantic: upwardly rather than downwardly mobile young people seeking better opportunities for themselves and their children. . . .

American rural communities have rarely been populated by the permanent, hidebound settlers that urban journalists and novelists have so condescendingly assumed. Southwestern farmers in the early twentieth century were highly mobile people who felt free to move about in search of better land or even to leave the land for opportunities in town. At the 1930 Census, forty-four percent of Oklahoma farmers and forty-seven percent of those in Arkansas said they had been on their current farms for less than two years. They were actually more mobile than the national farm average, where only twenty-eight percent answered the same. A 1937 study by a sociologist found that the average Oklahoma farmer moved four times in his working life, five times if he was a tenant. The Joads, who had all grown up in the same place where Grampa had fought off snakes and Indians in the nineteenth century, would have been most unusual Oklahomans.

A large part of Steinbeck's success with his reading public lay in his ability to merge deep, mythical concerns with the American experience. One of the reasons why his Okie story defined the era, while other Depression tales of poverty and hardship did not, was its theme from Exodus. But, once more, this part of the tale had very little historical authenticity. The road the migrants took was not a Biblical camel track but the comparatively new national highway Route 66, which since the 1920s had provided a direct route from the southwest to the California coast. Steinbeck treats the road more like covered wagon trail than the fast, modern highway it actually was. In reality, if their car was in good shape, an Oklahoma family in the 1930s could make it to California in three days. Rather than taking weeks while yarning about their hardship with other travellers and singing folk songs around campfires, the real migrants slept en route in auto courts (motels) for two or three nights. . . .

Real Migrants Had More Choices

Gregory points out that farming families had a number of options to make money en route. Some of them planned their journey to coincide with the Arizona cotton-picking season. Others who were less well organized nonetheless found plenty of agricultural employment along the way in the newly developed irrigation fields of the desert state. In the 1930s, Arizona acquired thousands of new citizens in this way.

This version of the story, in which agricultural migrants had many more active choices than the powerless victims of Steinbeck's novel, was also true of California. Although the state was hit particularly hard by the Depression, with the unemployment rate reaching twenty-nine percent in early 1933, its economy bounced back comparatively quickly between 1934 and 1937. In this period, Californian agriculture suffered not unemployment but labor shortages. . . .

California also had a much more generous unemployment relief system: $40 a month for a family of four, compared to $10 to $12 a month in the southwest. Although paying relief to migrants generated resentment among California taxpayers, it was an important consideration for agricultural workers. . . .

Most Okies Migrated Successfully

Rather than a tragedy, the Okie migration was a success story by almost any measure. By 1940, well before the World War II manufacturing boom transformed the Californian economy, a substantial majority of Okies had attained the goals that had brought them west. Eighty-three percent of adult males were fully employed, a quarter in white-collar jobs and the rest evenly divided between skilled, semi-skilled, and unskilled occupations. About twenty percent earned $2,000 or more a year, a sum that elevated them to middle-class status after less than five years in their new state. While their average incomes were beneath those of longer-established Californian families, their earnings were significantly higher and their unemployment rate significantly lower than that of their compatriots who remained in the southwest. In short, despite the Depression, California delivered on its promise.

It should be emphasized, however, that the received story of the great Okie Exodus was not entirely an invention. Instead of Steinbeck's 300,000, there were actually about 90,000 agricultural workers fitting the Okie category who migrated to and settled in Californian farming valleys in the 1930s. While the great majority of them prospered, a small minority did not. In 1937, when the problem of migrant homelessness was at its worst, a Californian government health survey estimated there were 3,800 of these families living in squatter villages of the kind portrayed in *The Grapes of Wrath*. This would appear to be the most accurate estimate of the number of people who experienced what the Joads went through. This is not an insignificant number, but neither is it a quantity that warrants being the received image of the Great Depression. This number amounted to about five percent of the dimension claimed by Steinbeck and gives a fair idea of the scale of exaggeration his book has perpetrated.

Steinbeck Helped Change Perceptions of the Homeless

Christina Sheehan Gold

Christina Sheehan Gold reviews books that focus on historical treatment of political and social issues.

In the following viewpoint, Gold states that activists worked to change the perception of the homeless in California in the 1930s, the era in which The Grapes of Wrath *was published. Advocates had to counter long-standing beliefs and fear about the homeless as dangerous outsiders. To combat these perceptions, supporters—including Hollywood celebrities and social workers—portrayed the homeless as hardworking pioneers who held traditional American values. Gold explains that, in* The Grapes of Wrath, *Steinbeck adopted the strategies of homeless advocates in the characteristics assigned to the fictional Joad family. Steinbeck helped to force the issue of homelessness and social welfare into the forefront of public discussion. As a result, the American public's perception of homelessness was altered, and support for helping the migrants became politically acceptable.*

In November 1939 eighteen cars full of people from the San Francisco Bay Area journeyed to California's San Joaquin Valley where they joined a similar contingent from Southern California. Newspaper advertisements boasted that participants in this quasi-tourist caravan would see the squalor and the poverty of California's agricultural migrants, visit squatters' settlements and government camps, and speak directly with homeless agricultural migrants. Carey McWilliams, Chief of

Christina Sheehan Gold, "Changing Perceptions of the Homeless: John Steinbeck, Carey McWilliams and California during the 1930's," in *Beyond Boundaries: Rereading John Steinbeck*, edited by Susan Shillinglaw and Kevin Hearle, Tuscaloosa: The University of Alabama Press, 2002, pp. 47–65. Copyright © 2002 The University of Alabama Press. All rights reserved. Reproduced by permission.

the California Division of Immigration and Housing, organized the trip, calling it a "See For Yourself" caravan as a challenge to those who disputed the accuracy of the depictions of migrant life in John Steinbeck's controversial novel, *The Grapes of Wrath*. At the end of their tour, the caravaners reported that Steinbeck was accurate and that government assistance to the migrants was necessary. Five months later, [First Lady] Eleanor Roosevelt embarked on a similar, well-publicized trip through California. She was accompanied by the popular actors Melvyn Douglas and Helen Gahagan, drawing further attention to the event. The First Lady and her small Hollywood entourage toured from Bakersfield to Visalia visiting the homeless. In public speeches the First Lady described the deplorable migrant conditions, reaffirmed Steinbeck's accuracy, and adamantly advocated for federal assistance to the homeless. . . .

The migrants [are] part of a long history of transient homelessness in America. Very old beliefs about homelessness, inherited from the British, informed Californians' perception and treatment of homeless migrants from the Southwest. Placing the migrants in the broad context of American homelessness helps explain Californians' reaction to them and illuminates a shift in American conceptions of the homeless.

Advocates Portrayed Homeless as Hardworking

Homeless advocates in California during the 1930s combated traditional perceptions of the homeless as dangerous outsiders and thrust into the public consciousness a new view of California's homeless migrants as hardworking pioneers and farmers who cherished traditional American values. Homeless advocates attempted to re-educate the public about homelessness in order to argue for social welfare. John Steinbeck's fictional account of the migrants, *The Grapes of Wrath* (1939), and Carey McWilliams's factual account, *Factories in the Field* (1939), adopted the methods established by homeless advocates. These important books threw the advocates' agenda full force into the public consciousness, propelled a shift in perceptions of the homeless, and enhanced public support for related social welfare.

Attitudes Inherited from British

Historians often trace American anxiety about the homeless far back to England between the fourteenth and seventeenth centuries when social and political changes created a growing homeless transient population. The devastating plague, the enclosure movement, a population boom, and a surge in unemployed soldiers created an unprecedented number of transients. The British blamed homeless transients for contributing to the economic and social turmoil that threatened the stability of feudal life, and they responded to the rise of transiency with measures that criminalized and stigmatized the homeless. . . .

The United States inherited, perpetuated, and even enhanced the British fear of homeless transients and the laws that punished them. These inherited attitudes and laws played a central role in shaping the ways that depression-era Californians responded to agricultural migrants from the Dust Bowl. . . .

Californian laws reflected and intensified a growing fear of homeless migrants, who came to symbolize the chaos caused by the severe economic depression.

Fear in California During the Depression

The fear of homeless outsiders coalesced around the simple belief that migrants would victimize local residents because they had no investment in the community. . . .

Californians perceived the homeless migrants as unknown outsiders with a propensity towards radical politics, contagious disease, welfare dependency, and immoral behavior.

Californians worried that the migrants were fertile soil for communist and socialist agitators. Waves of agricultural strikes fueled the belief that migrants were radicals, and public commentary revealed a fear that migrants might destroy a season's crops by striking during the harvest. Accusations of migrant political radicalism were often aimed at government camps where communism supposedly festered. . . .

Along with radical politics, residents accused the migrants of spreading disease and parasites. Migrant children, residents worried, would infect local children through contact at school. . . .

Many residents also believed that lazy migrants came to California to freeload off relief payments. . . .

In addition to being welfare dependents, migrants were perceived as immoral, ignorant, and even subhuman people, whose values and lifestyles were antithetical to those of their settled neighbors. . . .

Re-creating the Image of Homelessness

Homeless advocates, including social workers, government officials, artists, and local residents, struggled to redefine the public conception of homeless transients in order to increase empathy for the homeless and public support for social welfare. This new perception of the homeless blended romantic imagery with an emphasis on the structural causes of homelessness. The advocates' work involved an informal agenda, including five major tactics that challenged fearful attitudes.

First, nostalgic descriptions created by advocates likened the migrants to the courageous pioneers that settled the West. . . .

By associating the migrants with a familiar and admired American archetype, advocates combated perceptions of the homeless as dangerous outsiders.

Second, advocates cast the migrants as another favorite character from American history—Jeffersonian small farmers. They lamented a lost agrarian myth in romantic depictions of migrants as noble small farmers displaced from their land by cruel economic and natural forces. . . .

Third, advocates appealed to xenophobia and racism, frequently using the term "pure American stock" to contrast the Dust Bowl migrants with the workers from Japan, China, the Philippines, and Mexico, who had harvested California's crops in the previous decades. . . .

Fourth, homeless advocates strenuously argued that migrants were not lazy welfare dependents, but hard workers who were victims of misfortune beyond their control. Appealing to fairness and the Protestant work ethic, advocates explained that public assistance was justified because the migrants worked hard and lived simple honest lives, yet they were impoverished nevertheless. . . .

Fifth, and finally, advocates strenuously maintained that migrants were not political radicals or social misfits that endangered local communities. Migrants, advocates said, fulfilled an essential economic function, and they held deeply conservative political and social beliefs. . . .

Steinbeck and McWilliams

The public discussion of California's migrants heightened considerably, reaching national levels in 1939 with the publication of *The Grapes of Wrath* and *Factories in the Field*. These books complemented one another nicely, with McWilliams providing an objective, quantified analysis and Steinbeck providing a subjective, fictional account. Steinbeck tugged at the heartstrings, while McWilliams logically explained the problem.

John Steinbeck clearly adopted the homeless advocates' agenda. His understanding of the migrants was shaped in large part by his work and friendship with Tom Collins, a manager of a government camp for migrants. Collins, a homeless advocate, toured Steinbeck through the San Jaoquin Valley, imparting his understanding of the migrants in a way that

A farmer and his sons endure the Dust Bowl in 1936 Arkansas. AP Images.

paralleled the advocates' agenda. Prior to writing his epic novel, Steinbeck read through Collins' weekly camp reports to supply material for his story and characters. In those reports, Collins described the migrants as hard workers. . . . Collins' migrants were patriotic white Americans who yearned for the opportunity to once again farm their own land. . . .

Conversations with Collins and research for "The Harvest Gypsies" [a series of articles Steinbeck wrote for the *San Francisco News*] provided Steinbeck with the foundation for *The Grapes of Wrath*.

The Grapes of Wrath portrayed Okie migrants as part of a long tradition of pioneering into the state. Steinbeck did not romanticize the tradition, however, and described the pioneering migrants as "a horde of tattered feverish Americans" who were "hardened, intent, and dangerous." The earliest pioneering was born of a desperation that led the men to ruthlessly wrest the land away from its occupants. Even though Steinbeck criticized pioneering, the Joads, nevertheless, were part of this American tradition.

Furthering the advocates' agenda was Steinbeck's depiction of the Joads as Jeffersonian small farmers who were pitifully detached from their land and homes. The migrants, as opposed to California's commercial growers, were "true" farmers who shared a spiritual and physical attachment to the land. . . .

The displaced migrants had lived on the land for generations: "We measured it and broke it up. We were born on it, and we got killed on it, died on it. Even if it's no good, it's still ours. That's what makes it ours—being born on it, working it, dying on it." The novel bemoaned the loss of this connectedness with the land as banks, agribusinesses, and tractors dominated agriculture in the state.

The Grapes of Wrath alluded to issues of race, social welfare, and family values in ways that also mirrored the advocates' agenda. Although the novel did not use the term "pure American stock," or slander the minority workers, it repeatedly emphasized the migrants' American heritage. Steinbeck's fictional migrants described their ancestry: "We ain't foreign. Seven generations back Americans, and beyond that Irish, Scotch, English, German. One of our folks in the Revolution, an' they was lots of our folks in the Civil War— both sides. Americans." In addition, the Joads were by no means lazy welfare recipients who drained local budgets. The Joads' strong work ethic compelled them to leave the comfort of the government camp and return to their degrading, underpaid employment. In fact, the farmers benefited financially from the exploitation of their labor. The strength of family and community pervaded Steinbeck's book as Ma Joad struggled desperately to keep her family intact.

Finally, like the advocates, Steinbeck illustrated that migrant radicalism was born of poverty and social injustice. This radicalism would fester as a threat to the settled community unless the problem were repaired. Tom Joad described his emerging political philosophy:

> "I been thinkin' a hell of a lot, thinkin' about our people livin' like pigs, an' the good rich lan' layin' fallow, or maybe one fella with a million acres, while a hunderd thousan' good farmers is starvin'. An' I been wonderin' [what would happen] if all our folks got together an' yelled." The government camps provided a welcome amelioration of conditions, but Tom explained that they were not enough:

> I been thinkin' how it was in that gov'ment camp, how our folks took care a theirselves, an' if they was a fight they fixed it theirself; an' they wasn't no cops wagglin' their guns, but they was better order than them cops ever give. I been a-wonderin' why we can't do that all over. Throw out the cops that ain't our people. All work together for our own thing—all farm our own lan'.

The novel warned that the suffering caused by an unjust system would push the migrants to rebel against that system in order to achieve their traditional dream—to farm their own land.

Steinbeck gave sympathetic faces to an anonymous and frightening population, helping advocates combat the fear of migrants as dangerous outsiders. The Joad family personalized the homeless for readers who became intimately acquainted with the fictional migrant family's plight. The Joads and their situation became synonymous with the larger migrant condition. . . .

Advocates used the detailed and sympathetic descriptions of migratory life in the novel to support their pleas for enhanced public welfare. In the debate over federal camps, advocates pointed to Steinbeck's depiction of a government camp as a virtual oasis in a desert of poverty and deprivation. An article in the *Public Welfare News* described the gradual acceptance of federal camps and the key role of Steinbeck's novel:

> Gradually the program [government camps] has received community acceptance. . . . Economists, sociologists, and labor groups have seen the program meet problems for which there were not other solutions. And finally, John Steinbeck has produced his masterpiece, *"The Grapes of Wrath,"* which has made the nation aware both of the problem and of the successful if not entirely satisfactory way in which the Administration's program has at least ameliorated the living conditions of thousands of terribly underprivileged farm labor families.

Positive and Negative Reactions

The *San Francisco News* attributed legislative gains made on behalf of the migrants to Steinbeck's novel. "The magnitude of the program to date, and the prospect of further increase, can be largely credited to John Steinbeck's epic, 'The Grapes of Wrath.'"

In order for advocates to most effectively use *The Grapes of Wrath*, an essential question needed to be answered—did it accurately describe migrant conditions? Conservatives strenuously argued that the Joads were a complete fabrication, bearing no resemblance to real life. Carey McWilliams's book, *Factories in the Field*, gave advocates the proof they needed to counter these claims. Public commentary supporting *The Grapes of Wrath* repeatedly quoted facts and statistics drawn from *Factories in the Field*. Given Steinbeck's firm refusal to enter the public discourse about his novel, McWilliams became a primary spokesperson defending the accuracy of *The Grapes of Wrath*. This made sense not only because of the contemporaneous publication of McWilliams's book, but also because of McWilliams's position as the Chief of the Division of Immigration and Housing (DIH), which inspected migrant living conditions. In newspaper articles, public speeches, and radio broadcasts, McWilliams vehemently defended Steinbeck's novel against accusations of inaccuracy, propaganda, and vulgarity. Philip Bancroft, the Director of Public Relations for the Associated Farmers, charged that *The Grapes of Wrath* was "straight revolutionary propaganda." In response, McWilliams argued that his DIH inspectors found many Hoovervilles as miserable as the one Steinbeck described and that he had seen the handbills advertising work in California that had been distributed, out of state to attract migrants. In the *New Republic,* McWilliams acknowledged that factual evidence from his own work helped convince the public that *The Grapes of Wrath* was accurate. . . .

McWilliams and Steinbeck garnered intense hostility from conservatives. Congressional Representative Lyle Boren charged that *The Grapes of Wrath* "exposes nothing but the total depravity, vulgarity, and degraded mentality of the author." The Associated Farmers called Steinbeck an "arch enemy, defamer and slanderer." McWilliams was labeled "Agricultural Pest Number 1," and a farmer accused him of publishing propaganda rather than facts, saying that "there are other propagandists besides Messrs. Hitler, Stalin and Mussolini. And some of them live and publish their works right in America." Aside from angering conservatives, *The Grapes of Wrath* and *Factories in the Field,* guided by the advocates' agenda, drew a massive amount of interest to California's migrants, who could no longer simply be dismissed as criminals and welfare dependents. . . .

A New View of the Homeless

The massive amount of public attention and media focus on the migrants revealed the emergence of a new perception of the homeless that aligned with the advocates' agenda and broke away from the fear and disdain that had historically dominated Americans' feelings about the homeless.

Social Issues in Literature

CHAPTER 3

Contemporary Perspectives on Industrialism

Corporations and the Government Must Protect Farm Workers' Rights

Human Rights Watch et al.

Human Rights Watch is an international organization dedicated to protecting the rights and freedoms of people around the world. Its colleague organizations that joined it in signing the following letter also work for these goals.

According to Human Rights Watch and eight other organizations, agricultural workers in Florida are subjected to poor working conditions, low wages, lack of access to health care and, in some cases, forced labor and slavery. In a letter to the Organization of American States, which promotes social and economic development in the Western Hemisphere, a coalition of nine human rights organizations, including Human Rights Watch, Oxfam America, and Amnesty International, urges the United States government to take action against these human rights violations. The authors assert that the private sector, both growers and corporate purchasers of agricultural products, should be held accountable if they knowingly profit from these abuses.

The undersigned organizations submit this letter amici [in the capacity of friendly advisers] regarding the question of corporate and government responsibility for the poor human rights conditions of agricultural workers in Florida. The human rights of Florida's farm workers are under serious threat because of:

Forced labor and slavery: More than 1,000 agricultural workers in Florida have been subjected to forced labor and sla-

Human Rights Watch et al., "Letter to Santiago A. Canton, Executive Secretary, Inter-American Commission on Human Rights," http://hrw.org, March 2, 2005. Reproduced by permission.

very. [The] United States has criminally prosecuted these crimes under federal laws in six successful cases over the past seven years [prior to 2005], resulting in the sentencing of individuals to prison terms as lengthy as fifteen years. Despite these welcome efforts at enforcement, ongoing investigations by the U.S. Department of Justice indicate that agricultural workers in Florida continue to work under slavery and forced labor conditions.

Poor working conditions and lack of access to health care: Approximately 83 percent of agricultural workers nationally have no health care coverage. Most also work excessive hours, suffer increased injuries due to the physically demanding nature of their work, and are routinely exposed to dangerous toxins.

Low wages: The wages of agricultural workers in Florida are insufficient to guarantee the preservation of health and well-being. Agricultural workers in Florida earn from U.S. $2,500 to U.S. $7,500 on average per year, depending on a number of factors, including immigration status. Even if a worker picks tomatoes (a common crop in Florida) at the standard pace during a 12 hour day, he or she would harvest daily at least over 1 [frac12] tons and earn U.S. $50 per day, which amounts to an annual full time salary of U.S. $8,000. The poverty line in the United States for 2004 was defined by the U.S. Department of Health and Human Services as U.S. $9,310 for a single-person household. Therefore, such wages are far from sufficient for workers to access decent housing and other necessities.

The United States government should fulfill its responsibilities to protect agricultural workers in Florida from human rights violations and take steps to prevent further violations. The private sector, in particular the corporate sector, should comply with the law as well as recognize its role in ensuring that the human rights of its workers are respected. The U.N. Norms on the Responsibilities of Transnational Corporations and other Business Enterprises with Regard to Human Rights, which remain under study and are not binding, but do represent evolving standards within international law, state:

> Within their respective spheres of activity and influence, transnational corporations and other business enterprises have the obligation to promote, secure the fulfillment of, respect, ensure respect of and protect human rights recognized in international as well as national law.

In 2002 a federal court presiding over the Florida slavery cases pointed to the unique capacity of corporations to protect human rights. Judge Moore of the U.S. Southern District Court of Florida, referring to corporate actors, stated that "there are others at another level in this system of fruit-picking, at a higher level, that to some extent are complicit in one way or another in how these activities occur." The concentration of buying power among a small number of corporate purchasers of agricultural products in Florida makes them uniquely positioned to use their influence to demand greater respect for farm workers' rights and improved working conditions for farm workers in that state. The Coalition of Immokalee Workers (CIW) has called on them to do so.

While purchasing corporations are well-positioned to influence the human rights situation in the agricultural sector in Florida, the obligation to respect and ensure rights primarily resides with the U.S. government. Currently, the U.S. government has a discriminatory scheme for labor protection that excludes farm workers from the National Labor Relations Act, denying them protection for exercising their right to organize and form unions. Similarly, unlike most workers, farm workers are not guaranteed overtime pay under the Fair Labor Standards Act (FLSA). Moreover, even existing minimum wage and workplace safety protections, found respectively in the FLSA and the Occupational Safety and Health Act (OSHA), are severely under-enforced, contributing to the poor working conditions in Florida's agricultural sector.

While the United States has rightly pursued prosecutions for forced labor and slavery, it also must take action to prevent such violations. Prevention requires addressing discrimination and ensuring basic economic and social rights. It also requires allowing agricultural workers who have suffered human rights violations to switch employers without facing immigration consequences and the development of legislative and other mechanisms for ensuring corporations are held accountable (ideally both growers and purchasers) if they knowingly profit from severe human rights abuses such as slavery and forced labor.

As an important first step to address this situation, we call on the Commission to investigate these conditions among agricultural workers in Florida through site visits and further reporting. Secondly, we urge the Commission to ask the government of the United States to consider measures such as eliminating discrimination against farm workers in existing labor laws, granting workers who face serious abuses in their workplaces the opportunity to switch employers without immigration repercussions, and holding corporate purchasers accountable for knowingly purchasing products that were produced under conditions amounting to one of the most egregious human rights violations—slavery and forced labor.

Corporations Must Adhere to a Code of Ethics in the Post-Enron Environment

David F. Jadwin

David F. Jadwin is chairman of the Department of Pathology at Kern Medical Center in Bakersfield, California. He founded Columbia Healthcare Analytics, a Web-based company.

According to David F. Jadwin, many industries have experienced scandals and corporate collapse as a result of ethics-challenged management. Enron is the poster child for such corporate fiascos. Making ethical decisions is not always easy, Jadwin acknowledges, and sometimes the distinction between right and wrong is not clear, especially if the individual does not have the skills necessary to navigate moral challenges. The concept of ethical fitness has been developed to help individuals—and in turn the corporation they direct—meet ethical dilemmas. People cannot depend on regulators to define ethics for them, Jadwin asserts, since some behaviors are unenforceable. By adhering to and living five core moral values—honesty, respect, responsibility, fairness, and compassion—individuals can gain the moral courage to make ethical choices.

Everyone is familiar with the cancerous moral meltdown that arose in Enron's business culture. Fewer are likely aware that the Chernobyl power plant disaster resulted from a meltdown of ethics by Soviet engineers. The former wiped out billions from pension plans and investors and decimated thousands of jobs; the latter has an untold number of victims.

There is no shortage of similar instances: the Arthur Anderson scandal collapsed one of the most trusted accounting firms in the world; a broken safety culture at NASA led to the *Columbia* [shuttle] disaster: and pesticide leakage at a Union Carbide chemical plant in Bhopal, India, led to 20,000 deaths, devastating environmental contamination, and millions of crippling health problems for future generations. As one Bhopal survivor commented, the lucky ones were the people who suffered quick deaths. Each day politicians, soldiers, executives, and other employees are disgraced by career-ending consequences arising from questionable behavior.

The laboratory industry has faced its share of meltdowns—episodes of unethical Pap-testing, fraudulent testing strategies, transfusion-related hepatitis resulting from "cost-effective" screening, and in 2004, the release of thousands of HIV tests conducted at Maryland General Hospital without adequate quality control. These public disgraces are among many silent and seemingly lesser moral lapses that can occur in institutions with ethical apathy.

Making Ethical Decisions Is Not Always Easy

Meltdowns stem from impaired "right vs. wrong" decision making that leads to wrong moral choices. But ethical decision making is not always easy. The distinction between "right" and "wrong" is not necessarily obvious to the person making the decision, especially if he lacks the skills necessary to satisfactorily resolve treacherous moral challenges. Rushworth Kidder, founder of the Institute for Global Ethics, has developed the concept of "ethical fitness" a term that describes the capability of individuals to successfully meet ethical challenges.

Moral challenges range in spectrum from *clear* "right vs. wrong" choices to *uncertain* "right vs. right" dilemmas. Between these polar extremes lies an expansive zone, not clearly black or white, yet possibly appearing black or white depending upon the actor's set of values. It is commonly the values of individuals and institutions that govern how we re-

Laid-off Enron workers gather outside the company's offices. The Enron scandal, which involved the revelation of fraudulent accounting practices and the company's subsequent bankruptcy, highlighted the need for corporate codes of ethics. © Reuters NewMedia Inc./Corbis. Reproduced by permission.

spond—or fail to respond—when confronted with conflicts originating within this zone of uncertainty.

Individuals Must Be Ethically Fit

"Right vs. wrong" actions are sometimes regulated by law, but there are not enough regulatory resources, governmental or private, to police every decision, action, or outcome. Consequently, society relies upon ethics to "regulate the unenforceable" behavior of its members. Therefore, it is incumbent upon individuals and organizations to be ethically fit in order to meet emerging challenges. Establishing core values, living our core values, training our ethical-fitness muscles to respond appropriately when ethical challenges arise, and fostering moral courage develop "ethical fitness."

Research conducted by Dr. Kidder at his global-ethics institute has identified from dozens of values five core moral values—honesty, respect, responsibility, fairness, and compassion—that are shared universally by cultures around the world. But it is not enough to *have* core values. A copy of Enron's "Code of Ethics" was reportedly sold, unopened, on eBay. We must also *live* these core values.

Challenges present themselves as one or more of the following conflicts: truth vs. loyalty, community vs. individual needs, long-term vs. short-term goals, and the need for justice vs. mercy. These conflicts hearken back to issues involving core moral values of honesty, respect, responsibility, fairness, and compassion. Outcomes will depend upon the resolution principle selected to manage the conflict: end-based, rules-based, or care-based thinking.

In his book *Moral Courage*, Dr. Kidder writes "The importance of moral courage appears most vividly by its absence." Meltdowns, with consequential suffering, occur when the commitment to ethics and moral courage is lacking. Courage to act was apparently absent at Maryland General Hospital until, too late, an ethics-driven whistleblower stepped forward.

Ethical Fitness Relies on Moral Courage

Members of [the medical] profession should be mindful at all times of the perils arising from seemingly inconsequential actions that on the next day might appear in *The Baltimore Sun* or *The Wall Street Journal*. Whistleblowers, acting with moral courage, are ever present and growing in number. Ethical fitness is essential for personal and professional survival and is vital to safeguard patients and the reputation of any organization. With nuclear and industrial disasters, business and healthcare scandals, squandering of global resources, growing human poverty, and terrorist threats abounding, we should thoughtfully reflect upon Dr. Kidder's chilling prophecy: "We will not survive the 21st century on the ethics of the 20th century."

Industrialism Is Killing the Family Farm

Circle of Responsibility

Circle of Responsibility is a program of Bon Appétit Management Company that promotes a healthy environment, community, and socially responsible food choices. Bon Appétit Management Company is an onsite custom restaurant company that provides café and catering services to corporations, colleges and universities, and specialty venues.

According to the authors of the following viewpoint, the traditional pastoral image of the family farm is becoming a thing of the past. Industrial agriculture is pushing the small farms out of business. Federal legislation such as the Farm Bill of 2007 subsidizes commodities and plentiful, low-cost food grown via methods that the Circle of Responsibility asserts are harmful to the land and environment. Big agribusiness farms operate on the corporate model, which involves large-scale operations, extensive use of pesticides, and a single crop focus. Middlemen have entered the supply chain, further chipping away at the income available to small farmers. In the authors' view, industrial agricultural practices are unsustainable.

Rolling green pastures, golden wheat fields, healthy chickens and pigs happily scuttling around, a red barn in the distance: this is what most of us envision when we think of a traditional American farm. However, this idyllic image of the "family farm" is rapidly becoming an icon of the past. Due to advances in industrial agriculture over the past several decades, farms have become significantly larger and fewer in number, making it increasingly difficult for the small family farms to survive. In 2003, the farms and livestock operations

Circle of Responsibility, "Agribusiness and Family Farms," www.circleofresponsibility .com, 2007. Reproduced by permission.

Today's small farmers still struggle to make ends meet. Greg Forry, pictured in this 2005 photo, opened a farmers' market and bakery in order to survive. AP Images.

with annual sales of $250,000 or more represented only 8.8% of all farms in the U.S. but were responsible for approximately 73% of total farm sales. The remaining 27% of sales were divided up amongst the other 91.2% of smaller family farms.

What exactly is "agribusiness"? And what does it ultimately mean for us, the consumers?

Basically, "agribusiness" refers to businesses that are involved with agriculture. Although this may sound simple, it is actually quite complex. Agribusiness spans a wide range of sectors due to the multifaceted nature of our food system's supply chain. This includes all areas involved with food production, collection, storage, distribution, processing, and retail.

Quest for Efficiency Led to Industrialization

As each sector of the food supply chain strove for maximum efficiency, our agricultural system became more and more industrialized, shifting away from "small family farming." Coupling this increasingly economically driven food system with federal legislation like the [2007] Farm Bill (which subsidizes commodities) ultimately results in plentiful, affordable food for the consumer. And this is something that people in the US have come to expect. Compared to other high-income countries, Americans spend the least amount of their disposable income on food at home, about 6% compared to 10% in Germany and 13% in Japan, South Korea and France.

For agricultural traditionalists, "agribusiness" has come to mean the "fall of the family farm." Following such a "corporate" model takes farming and livestock production out of historical context and no longer differentiates these practices from other "big businesses." This industrialized system, they argue, encourages the farmer to be a businessman rather than a steward of the land. While these two goals are not mutually exclusive, they can be very difficult to balance.

Putting Smaller Farms Out of Business

Although this agribusiness boom has contributed to food security and the low cost of food in our country today, it is not without its detriments. Environmental damage such as water contamination, air pollution, soil erosion caused by large-scale operations (CAFOs), excessive pesticide use and monocropping have been well documented. Socially and economically, this industrialization has endangered what the Association of Family Farms calls the "agriculture of the middle." The few "big farms" are putting smaller farmers and ranchers out of business. Also, numerous middlemen have been introduced into the supply chain, which some people argue ultimately means less money for the farmer. Above all (and seemingly most obvious), continued industrialization of our agricultural system will significantly affect our food choices. Because most large farms practice monocropping (growing one type of crop) for "maximum efficiency," many heirloom varieties are being lost, meaning there are fewer and fewer flavors for us to enjoy.

Oil Shortages Will Change the Definition of Industrialism

John Michael Greer

John Michael Greer is the Grand Archdruid of the Ancient Order of Druids in America (AODA). Active in the alternative spirituality movement for more than twenty-five years, he is the author of a dozen books and lives in Ashland, Oregon.

Energy shortages will become the norm as oil production declines from its peak level, according to John Michael Greer. Greer suggests that the industrial society based on abundance will be forced to change to one focused on scarcity. The economic framework of the industrial world will no longer be sustainable, he asserts. Energy shortages will change the balance of global power toward governments willing to use military force to protect themselves and their resources. As fossil fuels become increasingly scarce, the industrial society will eventually become an "ecotechnic" society, which Greer defines as one which "relies on renewable energy resources, and maximizes the efficiency of its energy and resource use at the cost of far more restricted access to goods and services." Greer states that American attitudes need to change, and opposing forces must work together to develop constructive solutions if the nation is to survive an era of scarcity.

It's been suggested several times . . . that the process of coming to terms with the reality of peak oil has more than a little in common with the process of dealing with the imminence of death. The five stages of getting ready to die outlined by Elisabeth Kübler-Ross in a series of bestselling books back in the 1970s—denial, anger, bargaining, depression, and acceptance—show up tolerably often in today's peak oil controversies. There's good reason for the parallel, because the end

John Michael Greer, "The Age of Scarcity Industrialism," *The Archdruid Report*, October 17, 2007. Reproduced by permission.

of the age of cheap abundant energy marks the terminus of many of today's most cherished assumptions and ways of looking at the world, and it also means that a great many people alive today will die sooner than they otherwise would. . . .

Mass Consumption and Denial in the 1970s

When the diagnosis arrived at the beginning of the 1970s, for example, the immediate response was the one Kübler-Ross could have predicted: denial. By the end of that decade that response became an overwhelming political force. "It's morning in America," Ronald Reagan proclaimed, as his workmen tore down the solar hot water heaters Jimmy Carter installed on the White House roof: in some ways the definitive political act of the Eighties. Political gimmickry and reckless over-pumping of North Slope and North Sea oil fields forced the price of oil down to the lowest levels in history, and made it possible for the industrial world to wallow in one last orgy of mass consumption, the final blowoff of the Age of Exuberance.

Anger and Blame in the Late Twentieth Century

The next stage on Kübler-Ross's list, anger, arrived on schedule as the Eighties gave way to the Nineties. By the decade's end that stage, too, became a political force that put its poster boy in office, with a little help from hanging chads and the Supreme Court. The US invasions of Afghanistan and Iraq filled the same role in the new phase that the junking of the White House's solar panels filled in the old, a definitive sign that the new attitude held center stage in our national soap opera. It will be interesting to see whether the winning candidate in the 2008 election pursues a weak version of Bush II's policies, as Nixon did Johnson's and Bush I did Reagan's, and crashes and burns on schedule around 2012; history doesn't repeat itself, as the saying goes, but sometimes the rhymes are exquisitely precise.

One way or another, though, the stage of anger is fading out. Even oil company executives are starting to mention peak oil and global warming, and politicians are starting to tone down their rhetoric and climb aboard various bandwagons—ethanol, biodiesel, or what have you. This marks the arrival of bargaining. This stage has certain advantages; where denial refuses to deal with death, and anger looks for someone to blame for it, bargaining looks for things that can be done to make the Reaper change his mind. I've argued before that we're well past the window of opportunity in which the decline and fall of industrial society might have been prevented. Still, that doesn't foreclose the chance to cushion the decline and get things of value through the approaching mess, and these should be at the top of the industrial world's agenda right now.

Society Will Not Focus on Abundance

The first transition we face on the curve of the Long Descent ... will take us from a form of industrial society focused on abundance to another that centers on scarcity. It's a form without precedents outside of a few wartime examples, and the transition to it is likely to see a great many false starts and futile attempts to impose the thinking of the past on the realities of the future. Still, it's not an impossible transition, and will likely be easier than some of the others we'll face along the way.

The nature of the challenge is straightforward enough. The economic framework of the modern industrial world is geared to expansion: of goods and services, technology, energy use, resource extraction, and population, among other things. That won't continue as the limits to growth begin to bite in the next few years, and many things—starting with the economic framework of the industrial world—will have to change accordingly.

We're now close to two years past the peak of world oil production, and serious declines are likely to arrive in the next few years. How serious is a matter for guesswork today, but balancing failing production from existing fields against new production from fields under development and unconventional sources such as tar sands and biodiesel, something on the order of a 4% to 5% decline per year seems likely for the first decade or so. That will be a body blow to existing economic and social arrangements. Still, production increases of 4% to 5% a year didn't bring Utopia, and production declines on the same scale won't bring Armageddon, either.

Much Energy Use Is Wasted

A very large percentage of the energy used in a modern industrial society, after all, is wasted. During an age of cheap abundant energy, it's profitable to use energy in ways that have no real economic value at all, because the profit to be made selling the energy outweighs the short-term costs of wasting it. Tourism, the world's largest industry just now, is a classic example. Shut down the tourist industry—as every country in the world did during the Second World War—and redirect the resources now wasted on tourism to other uses, and industrial societies could weather a steep drop in energy supplies without impacting necessary goods and services. The same is true of many other dimensions of today's economy of waste.

In America, in particular, the sheer scale of energy waste makes phenomenal gains in efficiency fairly easy. The average American uses twice as much energy as the average Briton, and three times as much as the average European, to support a standard of living that by some measures is not even as high as theirs. Decades of shortsighted planning and inept economic policy will have to be undone in a hurry, as Americans discover that suburban living is no longer viable in a post-commuter age, but the problems involved aren't insuperable; for that matter, the rehabilitation of inner city neighborhoods and the rebuilding of mass transit systems could provide much-needed jobs to replace those lost when industries that exist solely to waste energy evaporate in the face of the new economics of scarcity.

Global Balance of Power Change

As this suggests, the fading out of the economy of waste promises to stand most of the economic slogans of the last two decades on their heads. When transportation accounts for most of the cost of many commercial products, that fact will write R.I.P. on the headstone of the global economy, because goods made overseas will be priced out of markets dominated by local production and regional trading networks. We've already begun to see the cutting edge of the new resource nationalism, as energy reserves and strategic raw materials become the mainsprings of political and military power, and governments start treating them accordingly. Expect this to expand dramatically in the decades to come, as dependence on foreign resources becomes a noose around a nation's neck and economic independence—even at a sharply lowered standard of living—the key to survival.

More generally, the pendulum of power could well swing away from the multinational corporations that have exercised so much influence in recent years, toward those national governments willing to use military force to maintain territorial integrity and control over resources. When most resource transfers across borders are negotiated between governments according to a calculus of political advantage, rather than being purchased on the open market by the highest bidder, those whose power comes solely from money will find themselves with a great deal less clout than they have today. Those governments that master the new calculus of power soonest, in turn, will dominate the age of scarcity industrialism.

The Ecotechnic Society

However it unfolds, the age of scarcity industrialism will no more be a permanent state of affairs than the age of abundance industrialism that precedes it. While it lasts, access to fossil fuels and other nonrenewable resources will be the key to international power and national survival, but by that very token fossil fuels and other nonrenewable resources will continue to slide down the curves of depletion. As resource production in one nation after another drops below levels that will support any kind of industrial system, industrial economies will unravel and give way to other forms of economy . . . in the process of succession that leads to the ecotechnic societies of the future.

What remains unknown is which of the current industrial societies will manage the transition to scarcity industrialism, and which will falter and crack under the strain. The United States could go either way. It's rare for a society that claws its way to the top of the heap under one set of economic conditions to hold onto that status when conditions change, and our society's fervent commitment to the economics of waste has opened up fissures of weakness throughout its economic, social, and political structure; the implosion of America's current empire is thus a foregone conclusion. If the next generation of American politicians are unusually lucky and smart, we might be able to coast down the curve of declining empire as Britain has. If not, we could face any of the usual fates of empire, ranging from stagnation and contraction to nightmare scenarios of political-military collapse and partition by hostile powers.

American Attitudes Need to Change

This is one reason why it would be useful for Americans on all points of the political spectrum to get over their habit of demonizing their opponents and wallowing in self-righteous anger as soon as possible, and start looking for constructive options instead. The time of bargaining, when preparations for the difficult future ahead of us can be made most readily, will not last forever. American culture always tends to extremes; the denial that blinded the Seventies and Eighties, and the anger that burst into incandescence in the Nineties and the present decade, were both of lavish dimensions. The phase of bargaining may well equal them; so, most likely, will the depression—economic, social, and spiritual—that comes when the efforts to bargain with the Reaper turn out to be too little and too late. We can only hope that when acceptance comes, it will be on the same grand scale.

Home Ownership Offers Security to Immigrants

Sue Kirchhoff

Sue Kirchhoff is an economics reporter for USA Today.

The current immigrant population in the United States—more than 30 million people—is gaining momentum as a force in the housing market. According to Kirchhoff, immigrants view home ownership as an important part of achieving the American Dream, providing security and the opportunity to become part of a stable community. Statistics reveal that immigrants are three times as likely as other adults to rank home buying as their top priority. However, affordability, lack of credit histories, and language and cultural barriers often challenge immigrants who pursue their dream. Kirchhoff states that many companies are changing their tactics in order to reach and assist the multicultural market.

Feng shui consultants are helping home builders connect with Asian clients. Home Depot has increased its Hispanic advertising budget. Real estate agents from Pennsylvania to rural Texas are enrolling in classes on cross-cultural marketing.

They're all reaching out to the more than 30 million immigrants in the USA who are an increasingly important factor in the housing market by revitalizing inner cities, changing the texture of suburbs and propelling subtle changes in home design.

Higher-than-expected immigration, both legal and illegal, is a major reason some economists expect the housing market to stay strong as mortgage rates rise from their lowest level in decades and the baby boomers begin retiring, putting homes on the market.

Foreign-born households bought nearly 8% of new homes and 11% of existing homes from 1998 to 2001. Immigrants were 12% of first-time home buyers in 2001 and buy more expensive homes on average than U.S.-born first-time owners, says the Harvard University Joint Center for Housing Studies.

While immigrants are concentrated in about a dozen large cities, including New York, Miami and Los Angeles, they are spreading out. Thirteen states had more than a 100% rise in their foreign-born population in the 1990s.

"It's security for my daughter, the security of owning the roof over your head," says Mislanys Rodriguez, 34, of Spring Hill, Fla.

With the help of Spanish-speaking mortgage brokers and real estate agents, Rodriguez and her husband, Angel, who came to the USA from Cuba in the mid-1990s, recently sold their starter house and moved to a larger home. Three of Angel's brothers own houses in the USA, as well. While immigrants are a growing presence, they lag behind the U.S.-born population by large margins when it comes to homeownership.

About half of immigrants own homes, compared with 70% of those born in the USA, a gap that closes as immigrants become U.S. citizens. The difference is also reflected in minority and white realty rates. About 47% of Hispanic and 49.7% of African-American households own their homes, compared with about 76% of whites. About 58% of Asian, Native American and Pacific Islander households are owners, says the National Association of Realtors.

"If I'm paying rent, I don't get any equity, I don't have a tax deduction, and the rent in San Francisco is just so high," said Giri Sastromihardjo, 34, an accountant who came from Indonesia in 1993.

He worked with Asian Inc., a San Francisco non-profit, and used government and private programs when buying his first home outside San Francisco.

A Growing Market

Corporate America sees huge potential in the immigrant market.

Former federal Housing and Urban Development secretary Henry Cisneros is now chairman and CEO of American CityVista, a joint venture with national builder KB Home, which constructs urban "villages" in big cities like Dallas, Fort Worth and Houston.

"We have yet to build a community that doesn't sell as fast as it can," says Cisneros, adding that one development in California was sold out at its groundbreaking.

"When we have a gap in the homeownership rate, that's more than just a gap in the honor of buying a house. That's a gap in the access to wealth," Cisneros says.

Real estate agents around the country report strong demand from foreign-born clients who see homeownership as the American dream. Immigrants are three times as likely as other adults to rank home buying as their top priority, says Andrew Schoenholtz, deputy director of the Georgetown University Institute for the Study of International Migration.

"They've struggled long enough. They have decent jobs. They want to leave a legacy for their kids," says Roberto Laureano, a real estate agent in Silver Spring, Md. "Go to settlement with a Hispanic family. You're not going to see just father and mom. You're going to see father and mom and the kids. They'll bring a camera. It means a lot."

The Affordability Barrier

But as prices rise, affordability is becoming a bigger barrier. Inability to speak English is a constant hurdle. Many foreign-born residents don't have credit histories. Discrimination is a factor.

Immigrants, on average, earn less but are clustered in some of the highest-priced housing markets in the country. Asians, however, have higher incomes on average than other ethnic groups. Another hurdle: An estimated 8 million to 10 million foreign-born people are in the USA illegally, lacking documents to get a mortgage.

"They are not easy loans by any means . . . you need to have a really good heart, a social service attitude toward your buyers," says Yamila Ayad, president of Mission Home Loans in San Marcos, Calif.

Some immigrants use backdoor methods to edge into the market, breaking the law and making them targets for exploitation. The Utah attorney general's office is investigating a scam involving up to 100 homes, many bought by illegal immigrants using stolen Social Security numbers.

Recent Census Bureau data show that Asian and Hispanic populations in the USA grew nearly four times as fast as the overall population from 2000 to 2003. There were about 39.9 million Hispanics in the USA in July 2003, nearly 14% of the population. Asians were the next-fastest-growing segment, at about 4.6% of the population.

"Any demographer in the state of Texas would tell you that in just a few short years . . . whites, or Anglos, will be a minority. That's coming to a neighborhood near you," says Gary Maler, associate director of the Real Estate Center at Texas A&M University.

The number of new households, key to housing demand, could be about 10% higher in the next decade than predicted, largely due to immigration, says the Harvard Joint Center for Housing Studies.

"It's had a very dramatic impact," says Eric Belsky, director of the Harvard Center. Housing experts had warned that the baby bust, a smaller generation after the baby boom population surge, would suppress household growth and demand for starter homes.

"That didn't really transpire," Belsky says. "While that baby bust (population) is still smaller than the baby boom, it's a lot less smaller than it would have been."

Some experts point out that immigrant homeownership rates declined in the 1990s, probably due to the sheer size of immigration during the decade, the highest since the late 1800s. But homeownership rates typically rise after immigrants have been in the country a period of years.

"We will see an increase in homeownership rates for immigrants over time. . . . In a decade, I think we may see that it's a significant increase," Schoenholtz says.

Closing the Housing Gap

Still, the non-profit Center for Housing Policy points out that 14% of immigrant families pay half their incomes for housing, vs. about 8% of U.S.-born families.

Politicians, sales agents, bankers and non-profit groups are trying to help close the housing gap, with everything from financial training to down-payment assistance.

The Congressional Hispanic Caucus, working with housing giant Fannie Mae and others, has created a housing program targeting congressional districts with large Hispanic concentrations. The League of United Latin American Citizens (LULAC) and GMAC Mortgage plan to provide more than $400 million in loans to Hispanic communities in the next four years.

Some banks are experimenting with loans using a federal tax identification number in lieu of a Social Security number. That could help immigrants who don't have legal documentation. The subprime market, loans to higher credit risks, is an important factor.

Asha Abokor, 36, from Somalia, recently bought a house in Phoenix. She used her own money and a rebate from KB Home for a down payment. Because she does not have a credit history, she is paying an above-market interest rate.

"I wanted it as an investment, to belong to a community with established roots. All those things were really important," Abokor says.

The National Association of Realtors, the National Association of Hispanic Real Estate Professionals and other groups have stepped up cross-cultural marketing.

Texas A&M's Maler surveyed more than 4,000 Texas residents about housing preferences. He found Asians were willing to spend more for a house than other groups. Blacks were more apt to visit neighborhoods before buying. Hispanics had the least experience with home buying, were likely to seek family advice and wanted a sales agent who speaks Spanish.

Omar Garcia started Aventa Real Estate Services in Tampa [in 2003], offering real estate, title insurance and mortgage service. He now has nearly 50 employees.

"Why would I open up a real estate company (now)? Rates are at an all-time low, going to go up. Impacts of technology are starting to affect the general real estate market, margins are getting thinner," says Garcia, whose firm helped the Rodriguez family.

But he says there are unmet needs in the Hispanic market, particularly in financing.

Home Depot is accelerating its efforts to reach the multicultural market. The home-improvement chain hired a new ad agency and significantly increased its Hispanic marketing budget. It sponsors the Mexican national soccer team, supports the Hispanic Chamber of Commerce and other groups.

Saul Gitlin, executive vice president for strategic marketing at Kang & Lee, a New York-based multicultural advertising firm, says participants at the National Hardware Show—firms selling products for the home—were intrigued when he laid out statistics about market clout of Asians in the USA. Though less than 5% of the population, Asians have the highest median home value in 48 states.

"The financial services industry ... are all over the Asian-American market like a bee on a flower," Gitlin says.

The Asian Real Estate Association of America cautions that many Asian immigrants need home-buying help. The group is conducting a study of income and education trends and needs within the Asian community.

"A house means the future of our family," Ayad says. "It's one of the greatest joys."

For Further Discussion

1. In Chapter 1, Peter Lisca describes how Steinbeck's personal observations in the migrant camps provided content for *The Grapes of Wrath*. Yet in Chapter 2, Charles Cunningham and Keith Windschuttle promote the view that Steinbeck exaggerated or misrepresented the living conditions, numbers, and treatment of the migrants. Why do you think such contradictory information exists? What might be influencing each writer's viewpoint? Discuss your conclusions about whether Steinbeck's portrayal of the Okies reflected reality and what information helped to form your conclusions.

2. Joseph Allegretti talks in Chapter 2 about how corporate moral standards, or lack of them, can cause people to override their own personal moral code, leading them to adopt behaviors they really don't believe in. Meanwhile, in Chapter 3, David F. Jadwin admonishes corporations to act ethically and responsibly, using the Enron debacle as an example of the failure to impose a code of ethics. What other current-day examples, where personal ethics were either adhered to or ignored in the corporate or political realm, can you think of? Have you had any personal experiences that required you to make a decision about your code of ethics versus someone else's expectations? How can individuals, such as the tractor men in *The Grapes of Wrath*, operate within the corporation without compromising their own values?

3. In Chapter 2, Christina Sheehan Gold states that Steinbeck and *The Grapes of Wrath* helped to change perceptions of the homeless for the better. How do you think the changes in attitude described in that viewpoint compare to percep-

tions of the homeless today? What similarities and differences can you identify between the "Okie" migrants and present-day homeless people?

4. In Chapter 1, Richard Astro describes how Steinbeck's formative years made him empathetic toward common people. Also in Chapter 1, Anders Österling references Steinbeck's contributions to portraying the struggles of ordinary people against external forces. Given Steinbeck's sympathies for the "underdog," do you think his depiction of the Okies, in particular the Joads, overlooked their weaknesses? Were the Okies responsible for their own problems? Why or why not?

5. Industrialism has delivered many changes and, some would say, improvements, to everyday life. People at one end of the spectrum, such as the immigrants discussed in Sue Kirchhoff's viewpoint in Chapter 3, strive to achieve the "American Dream" and the benefits of industrialism. But some view industrialism as a negative—the cause of environmental and social problems. For example, in Chapter 3, the Circle of Responsibility discusses its belief that industrialism will bring the ruin of the family farm. John Michael Greer asserts in Chapter 3 that declining oil supplies will usher in an era of scarce resources and less "abundance." Do you think there is a way to balance the perceived benefits of industrialism with preservation of the environment, concern for the individual, and adherence to traditional ways of life, such as family farms? Is it important to work toward such a balance or do Americans need to come to terms with the inevitability of change?

For Further Reading

Charles Dickens — *Hard Times*. England: Harper & Brothers, 1854.

James Hilton — *Lost Horizon*. London: Macmillan, 1933.

Sinclair Lewis — *Babbitt*. New York: Harcourt, Brace, 1922.

Horace McCoy — *They Shoot Horses, Don't They?* New York: Simon & Schuster, 1935.

Ayn Rand — *Atlas Shrugged*. New York: Random House, 1957.

Upton Sinclair — *The Jungle*. New York: Doubleday, Page, 1906.

John Steinbeck — *Cannery Row*. New York: Viking, 1945.

John Steinbeck — *In Dubious Battle*. New York: Covici-Friede, 1936.

John Steinbeck — *Of Mice and Men*. New York: Covici-Friede, 1937.

John Steinbeck — *Tortilla Flat*. New York: Covici-Friede, 1935.

Bibliography

Books

Richard Astro   *John Steinbeck and Edward F. Ricketts: The Shaping of a Novelist*. Minneapolis: University of Minnesota Press, 1973.

Susan F. Beegel, Susan Shillinglaw, and Wesley N. Tiffney Jr., eds.   *Steinbeck and the Environment: Interdisciplinary Approaches*. Tuscaloosa: University of Alabama Press, 1997.

Jackson J. Benson   *The True Adventures of John Steinbeck, Writer*. New York: Viking, 1984.

Timothy Egan   *The Worst Hard Time: The Untold Story of Those Who Survived the Great American Dust Bowl*. New York: Houghton Mifflin, 2006.

Thomas Fensch, ed.   *Conversations with John Steinbeck*. Jackson: University Press of Mississippi, 1988.

Warren French, ed.   *A Companion to "The Grapes of Wrath."* New York: Penguin, 1989.

Tetsumaro Hayashi, ed.   *John Steinbeck: The Years of Greatness, 1936–1939*. Tuscaloosa: University of Alabama Press, 1993.

Peter Lisca   *John Steinbeck: Nature and Myth*. New York: Crowell, 1978.

| Harry Thornton Moore | *The Novels of John Steinbeck: A First Critical Study*. Port Washington, NY: Kennikat Press, 1939; reissued, 1968. |

| Jay Parini | *John Steinbeck: A Biography*. New York: Henry Holt, 1995. |

| Roy Simmonds | *John Steinbeck: The War Years, 1939–1945*. Lewisburg, PA.: Bucknell University Press, 1996. |

| Elaine Steinbeck and Robert Wallsten, eds. | *Steinbeck: A Life in Letters*. New York: Viking, 1975. |

| John Steinbeck | *The Harvest Gypsies: On the Road to "The Grapes of Wrath."* Berkeley, CA: Heyday Books, 1996. |

Periodicals

| Eugene R. August | "Our Stories/Our Selves: The American Dream Remembered in John Steinbeck's *The Grapes of Wrath*," *University of Dayton Review*, winter 1995–1996, pp. 5–17. |

| William J. Beck and Edward Erickson | "The Emergence of Class Consciousness in *Germinal* and *The Grapes of Wrath*," *Comparatist: Journal of the Southern Comparative Literature Association*, May 1988, pp. 44–57. |

| Roxanne Dunbar-Ortiz | "One or Two Things I Know About Us—Rethinking the Image and Role of the 'Okies,'" *Queens Quarterly*, fall 1995, pp. 566–76. |

Economist	"It's Wise to Deindustrialise," April 26, 1997, p. 78.
Richard W. Fossey	"The End of the Western Dream: *The Grapes of Wrath* and Oklahoma," *Cimarron Review*, 1973, pp. 25–34.
Warren French	"John Steinbeck and American Literature," *San Jose Studies*, spring 1987, pp. 35–48.
Marc Grossman	"Chavez, Steinbeck; The Ties That Bind," *Sacramento (CA) Bee*, October 20, 2002.
Rebecca Hinton	"Steinbeck's *The Grapes of Wrath*," *Explicator* winter 1998, pp. 101–103.
Marci Lingo	"Forbidden Fruit: The Banning of *The Grapes of Wrath* in the Kern County Free Library," *Libraries and Culture*, fall 2003.
David Moberg	"Labor Fights for Rights," *Nation*, September 15, 2003, p. 24.
Jeffrey Pfeffer	"It's Time to Start Trusting the Workforce," *Business 2.0*, December 2006, p. 68.
Richard S. Pressman	"Them's Horses—We're Men: Social Tendency and Counter-Tendency in *The Grapes Of Wrath*," *Steinbeck Quarterly*, summer/fall 1986, pp. 71–79.

Walter Fuller Taylor	"*The Grapes of Wrath* Reconsidered: Some Observations on John Steinbeck and the 'Religion' of Secularism," *Mississippi Quarterly*, summer 1959, pp. 136–144.
Nicholas Visser	"Audience and Closure in *The Grapes of Wrath*," *Studies in American Fiction*, spring 1994, pp. 19 (18).
Ray Lewis White	"*The Grapes of Wrath* and the Critics of 1939," *Resources for American Literary Study*, autumn 1983, pp. 134–164.
Sol Zollman	"John Steinbeck's Political Outlook in *The Grapes of Wrath*," *Literature and Ideology*, 1972, pp. 9–20.

Index

as hardworking, 128–129
perceptions of, 127–137
Homestead Act, 113–114
Hoover, J. Edgar, 9
Howe, Julia Ward, 90, 104
Human actions, machines as
metaphors for, 82–83
Human failings, 53–54
Human rights violations, of farm
workers, 139–142
Human Rights Watch, 139
Humanity, common, 77–80

I

Idealism, 26
Immigrants
growth in numbers of, 158–
159, 161
home ownership for, 158–164
Industrial economy, 83–85
Industrial Valley (McKenney), 35
Industrialism
family farms and, 148–150
oil shortages and, 151–157
Interchapters, role of in distancing
readers, 51–52
Irrigation, 114
Israelites, 91–94, 100–101

J

Jadwin, David F., 143
Jeffersonian agrarianism, 54–55,
60, 65
Jim Casy (character)
as Jesus figure, 96–98
spiritual conversion of, 109
unity theme and, 24–26
as voice of socialism, 106–108
Joad family
biblical parallels with, 90–101

transformation of, 78–79,
102–109
was exaggeration, 120–126
John Joad (character), 96–97
John Steinbeck (Parini), 9
John the Baptist, 96–97
Judas, 95–96

K

Kidder, Rushworth, 145–147
Kirchhoff, Sue, 158
Kramer, Mark, 117–118
Kübler-Ross, Elisabeth, 151

L

L'Afaire Lettuceberg (Steinbeck),
32
Land
alienation of humans from,
114–115
conquest of, 113–114
consolidation of, 114, 117
human responsibility for erosion of, 56–57
relationship of migrants with
the, 57
Land of the Free (MacLeish), 35
Land ownership, in California,
115–117
Language, 34
League of United Latin American
Citizens (LULAC), 162
LeSueur, Meridel, 115
Life-instinct, 44–45
Lisca, Peter, 29, 90–91, 100
The Long Valley (Steinbeck), 23,
38

M

Machine motif, 81–89
Machines
humans displaced by, 115,
117–118